INTRODUCTION

The 1980s was a heady time for magic books. It was an explosion of information. It was also something of a personality parade as we got to better know seasoned magicians through the release of compilations of their work, and hear new voices in magic via the seemingly endless flow of publications. As the ability to record video became inexpensive (and omnipresent), the flood of information took the form of VHS tapes, then, when magnetic particles reached their life expectancy, DVDs. Books went the way of the white rhino – they continued to roam the earth, but in smaller numbers.

Those of us who were, and are, avid readers hold affection for books. In the 80s it felt like the new magic books were stuffed with ideas – it was a time of thoughts unchained. For many, the somewhat loose, loopy style of Paul Harris and others who published in the 70s and 80s is remembered as a point of departure. Those books often offered, in addition to tricks, a unique voice. The voice made itself known both in the scripting of the effects, and, at times, the nature of the effects themselves.

Jonathan Friedman has produced a book that would have been at home back then. His antic personality is as much a part of the whole as the effects he teaches – but the real finds are in the in-betweens, the details. As is true of the books he admires, one reads through the routines discovering elements that can be added to one's arsenal of solutions: a winning move here, an interesting approach or phase there. This is a book of tricks, yes, but more importantly a book of ideas from a voice we haven't heard from before.

Hello, Jonathan.

— **David Regal**

"We are the music makers...
and we are the dreamers of dreams."
-Willy Wonka

The 80's Called...
They Want Their
Magic Book Back

Volume One

Editing:
Michael Vance
Lisa Falk

Photographs:
Ben Sandall

Cover Design and Illustrations:
Marshall Fanciullo

Layout and Design:
Jeff Weiser

Published by Shades of Magic
www.shadesofmagic.com

Distributed By Murphy's Magic Supplies, Inc.

Printed and bound in the United States of America
First Edition

Jonathan Friedman

ACKNOWLEDGMENTS

To my beautiful wife Jennifer, who taught me the true meaning of the word "magic" the day that I met you.

To my most excellent kids Zoe and Jake, who despite my constant pushing have yet to completely appreciate the fine art of conjouring. It's not too late to join the family business, is it?

Thank you to my father Gary for first giving me the gift of appreciating magic. I hope that I carried your magic torch well. Thank you to my mother Timothea, for all of the years of support, love, and pretending to be fooled when you probably weren't. Also, sorry I almost shot your eye out while performing needle through balloon. It was all in the name of entertainment.

To my "other" parents, Barney and Peggy. Thanks for not losing your minds when I duped you into thinking that your daughter was simply marrying a musician, not a secret agent man of mystery. You both are tremendous people.

To my sister Lisa and brother Mychael. You both helped out massively in your own special ways. Thanks for not crying too loudly when it became very obvious that I was our parents' favorite.

To Joe Cole. Thank you for always taking the time to allow this overly-ambitious freak to bounce a bare minimum of at least twenty ideas off of you in a one-hour time slot. You are the best.

To Michael Fisher. We go way back. You even gave me my first job at a magic shop. Unpaid of course, but it was a job in show business. Can't complain about that.

To Darryl, Sheila, William, and Geoff. Thanks so much for making room for one more at the greatest magic shop in all the land, Market Magic Shop in Seattle, WA.

To Nash Fung, Samuel Shaefer, and Jack Carpenter. You guys welcomed me with open arms into the Seattle magic scene. Thanks so much for the stimulating conversations, enjoyable lunches and all of the laughs.

To Marshall Fanciullo, who is largely responsible for so many aspects of this book. Everything from working on illustrations, to brainstorming ideas, to keeping the "magic" alive, as well as providing the wonderful cartoon title blocks in this book. Marshall, you are a 100% class act and you still continue to give far too much of your time away to others.

To Jeff Weiser, my creative soul partner. Together, we've been through a tremendous stretch of goofing off, growing up, and hanging out. Your generosity never ceases to amaze me, not to mention your devilish eye for talent and all things hip.

To Ben Sandall, for taking some top-flight photos. You are a top-flight guy and I appreciate your help immensely.

To David Regal. The opportunity to be "introduced" to the magic community by one of my idols is something bigger than I am fully able to wrap my brain around at this time. You taught me the importance of a script. I was listening. Thank you.

To Stephen Minch. Your big, bad brain never ceases to amaze me, along with your willingness to lend a helping hand with credits when needed. It was definitely needed.

Thank you to Ian Kendall and Andi Gladwin, for so carefully writing up my very first published pieces. Thank you to both Richard Kaufman and Stan Allen for publishing my work in the finest magic magazines out there, as well as giving an unknown like me a break.

Thank you to Michael Vance and Lisa Falk for carefully making sense of these pages, as well as insisting that I start dotting my "I's" and crossing my "T's" and not the other way around.

A special thanks to John Guastaferro, Steve Mayhew, Cameron Francis, Francis Menotti, Shaun Dunn, Jack Carpenter, and Joe Cole. Your contributions, routines, and ideas really classed up this joint. I can't even begin to thank each and every one of you for being so generous with your material and for trusting me with delivering the goods. You allowed me to tweak, adapt, and script your contributions into routines that I simply just love to perform...all of the time. You are all amazing in my book, and anybody else's for that matter.

In a world chock full of DVDs, digital downloads, and free YouTube videos, who needs an actual, real-life magic book? Well, for starters, I do and since you have purchased this book, I'm going to assume that you also feel the same overwhelming "need to read". And for that, I truly thank you from the bottom of my page-turning, chapter-burning heart.

So, let's address the two obvious questions: What's the story behind the title of the book and really, what's up with the sunglasses? Well, since you asked, here goes. The 1980's were a very good time for me, magically speaking. It was during this glorious decade that I made the life-changing leap from department store, birthday present magic kits to purchasing shiny, yet sophisticated individual tricks from magic shops and catalogs. Add to this the very limited supply of general magic books available from the local library and I suddenly felt as if I had it all. My life was complete. An active library card and twenty or so gimmicked magical pieces of plastic and I was now ready to call myself a "man of magic", despite the fact that I was barely into my teens.

Age 12, wide-eyed and almost innocent.

What I did not know was that outside of this safety net I liked to call "my magic", there existed an entire world of cutting-edge magical routines that were overflowing with personality, wit, and new exotic sleight of hand techniques designed to accomplish the type of miracles that I could barely even wrap my mini sponge ball brain around. I really could have it all and all I had to do was begin to look in the right places. Fortunately, I was lent a book to read through. My world changed like a black card to red overnight with a few casual turns of the page. The book in question? *Supermagic* by Paul Harris (1977). This guy thought "different". His books read "different". He was "different"…and so was I. It was then I realized that "different" is good, which was a very radical concept for a teenager. I soon gobbled up every Paul Harris book I could get my hands on. In the 80's, this was easy. It seemed that books were growing on trees. I really did have it all. I could now link playing cards together, slide coins into and out of mirrors, and so many other brain-melting effects, all because some guy in Las Vegas decided to share his close-up fantasies with the world. I was listening, but more importantly, I was reading.

But there were others as well. I devoured whatever I could by Richard Kaufman, Ben Harris, David Harkey, Jay Sankey, David Regal, Michael Weber, Stephen Minch, and countless others as well. I was hooked. I was influenced. I was well-read. I was ambitious. Mix all of that together with a kid that possesses a lot of time on his hands and you set the stage for what was to become my very own magic book. This was what I wanted to do. I was going to do. I just had to do it.

Well, real-life did its crazy thing and I found myself very fortunately making my way through the world as a working musician, which is probably one of the most "magical" things in the world. What can I say? My priorities shifted. The opportunity to make music was very important at that point of my life and I was very lucky to have had it. That being said, I just didn't have the time to keep up with pursuing my magical dreams. It was the 90's and I had some Grungy Alternative Rock to do and so I did it. But here is the thing. When I wasn't tuning my guitar, I read. When I wasn't writing songs to sacrifice at the altar of the rock gods, I read. When I

Not a bad way to pay the bills. Magical in its own rockin' way.

was leaving my beautiful wife and two awesome kids at home to go play "hurry up and wait" at a gig, what did I do to pass the time and keep my sanity? I read. And that was enough…then.

Well, I closed my eyes and realized about twenty musically rockin' years had gone by and yes, they absolutely were filled with plenty of "magic". Life seemed pretty "conquered". What next?

Once the strings stopped vibrating and the fog machine dried up, I realized that it was time for my magical comeback/big debut. I was going to finally write that dang book. Well, I heard it from every corner. "Why don't you just make a DVD?" "You should just make some videos and put them online". "A book? What is this, the 80's?" I thought those suggestions over for about nine seconds and then answered a great big "Nope" to all of that nonsense. Bottom line is this. I like to read. I want to read. But most importantly, I want to write a book that I would want to read. And that is what this is.

Every single one of the routines in this book has been performed outside the comforts of my own little head. Now, let's get this straight. I do not actively do birthday parties, restaurants, or trade shows. That's not my scene. I'm that guy who stuffs his pockets up with a deck, some coins, and then hits the real world. Maybe my miracles occur "on the fly" in social gatherings. Maybe they pop up at work, when everyone should probably have been doing something "productive". Well, thank goodness I have always been there to put a stop to that. That's not to say that my material hasn't been tested and performed in the usual working magician's environments. It has. I am blessed to have a "posse" of magician-friends that have always been willing to try out my latest and greatest in those restaurant, party, and trade show situations that define one as a "working pro". But here's the thing. You don't have to be a "working pro" to act like a pro and that's what I have striven to do. I thought very hard and I worked extremely diligently on this book, in order to give my own brand of originality back so that hopefully it can be the catalyst in making somebody out there want to pick up another magic book and read it. To me, that's what a "pro" should want to do. I've given you plenty to think about in this book. I've even given you complete scripts to use, which I personally would love for you to try. Hopefully, by jumping in and trying out some of these routines, you can take your magic to the next level and be whatever kind of "pro" it is that you have always wanted to be.

Oh yeah and far as the sunglasses go, well, they pretty much just make me feel cool.

Jonathan Friedman

To Jonathan
What a magical man!
George Takei

Performing some of my magic for the legendary George Takai at Market Magic Shop in Seattle, WA.

CONTENTS

Effect

A booty-kicking, three-phase, "find-a-card" routine utilizing top-secret ninja techniques to get the job done. Playing cards are thrown, transformed, turned invisible, and the spectator even finishes the trick off by throwing this invisible "ninja star" card directly into the pack themselves, where it visibly appears right next to the selection. Inspired by "Stabbed In The Pack" by Johnny Benzais and Harry Lorayne (The Best Of Benzais, 1967), the origins of this type of effect go all of the way back to Gus Bohn's "Face Up Location" in Walter Gibson's *Two Dozen Effective Practical Card Tricks* (1927).

Featuring The Trashcan Production and Slap Trap: Two new moves to add to your ninja bag of tricks.

Needed

A deck of playing cards with a Joker.

Preparation

None

Performance

While keeping the face of the deck toward yourself, spread through it until you get to the Joker. Cut this Joker to the rear of the face-up deck and then turn the entire pack face down. The Joker is now the top card of the deck.

"Ya know, I didn't always want to be a magician. Growing up, I wanted to be a ninja. That's right, a ninja. I mean, who wouldn't want to be a ninja? Plus, I had an Uncle Bob who was a ninja and he was pretty cool, so...that's right, Uncle Bob the ninja. True story."

Give the deck whatever set of shuffles and false cuts that will make you happy, as long as you keep the Joker on top.

"As a kid, I wasn't able to go get the latest ninja weapons whenever I wanted like all the other cool ninja kids on the block. But I didn't have to. I learned to improvise with a deck of cards."

After shuffling the pack, hold it in left-hand dealer's grip and slide the bottom card out with your right thumb and first two fingers. Give this card a gentle 360-degree spin in the air, catching it with whichever hand that feels more comfortable. I always shoot for the hand holding the deck, but sometimes I do need to adjust on the fly and catch it with the right hand instead. Once the card has been caught, bury it back into the center of the pack.

"Who really needs throwing stars when you can use throwing cards?"

Pick up the deck in right-hand Biddle Grip and swing cut the top half of the cards into your left hand with your right index finger. You are going to re-grip the cards in your right hand by straddling their outer corners

fig. 1 fig. 2

with your right index finger and pinky (fig. 1). By increasing the pressure on these corners, you will be able to let go of the cards with your right thumb. Re-position your thumb to the center of the outer end of the cards and perform a face-down one-handed fan, bringing it up to chest level as you tilt your right hand back toward you, displaying the face of the card fan to the spectator.

"Who needs a fancy ninja fan from the Far East when you can just use a card fan?"

You are now ready to perform "The Trashcan Production", an original move that I have been performing for well over twenty-five years. It has its roots firmly planted in the Cardini Color Change, but here it is used as a production instead of a straight-ahead color change.

THE TRASHCAN PRODUCTION

Push over the Joker on top of the left half with your thumb and then pull it back, catching a pinky break underneath it. Everybody is looking at the fan at this time, so you are completed covered as you get your pinky break.

Both of your hands work in unison during this production. Lower the right hand's fan straight down so that it is about three inches directly over the top of the deck, tilted forward enough to cover the front edges of the cards in the left hand.

This fan will be providing a screen as the left hand levers the Joker up at a ninety-degree angle (like a trashcan lid), bringing it perpendicular with the rest of the deck (fig. 2, exposed side view). Make sure that you are holding the cards in dealer's grip, with the outer right corner of the deck gripped between the right index and middle fingers. The left hand's grip

fig. 3

fig. 4

is crucial to ensure that the card levers up smoothly, as well as in the correct position to be stolen back under the fan. To make this happen, you will simply be straightening out your left fingers, causing the face-up Joker to completely lever over to a horizontal position. As you tilt the fan back to its original position directly over the deck, the bottom two fingers of the right hand are freed to extend to the left to grab the card once it has been levered and revolved face up (fig. 3, from below).

"Let me actually introduce you to my very own ninja master. Here he is."

Wave the right-hand fan over the left hand in a small circle. Allow your left fingertips to contact the back of the face-up Joker and then slowly slide it out from beneath the fan (fig. 4)

"I know he looks like an average joker, but he is a real-life ninja master. He's dressed in black. He slices and dices his way through the darkness of the deck. He's the real deal."

Place the face-up Joker on top of the left hand's cards and then close the one-handed fan in your right hand. Place the cards in the right hand underneath everything in the left and you are ready to proceed.

Take the Joker into your right hand and give it a couple of spinning tosses toward the deck. Your goal is to catch it on top of the pack. This very well may be the most difficult part of the routine, for me at least. Just give it a spin toward the deck and then lift the left thumb off of the pack so that you can trap the Joker with it as it lands on top of the deck.

"Once I teamed up with the master, I got pretty decent with the throwing card, my weapon of choice. As a matter of fact, my friends even called me... The Wannabe (rhymes with wasabi) Ninja. Pretty cool. I didn't know what it meant. Wannabe. Probably means something like 'way of the warrior'. Then, I realized that I read it wrong; not Wannabe, Waaaaaaanabe (like 'wanna be')."

Adjust the face-up Joker so that it is squared with the rest of the deck in the left hand, if it didn't already land that way. If it did, you rule.

"Ouch. That's when I got angry, and when I got angry, I got good."

PHASE ONE (LETHAL ACCURACY)

Spread the cards from hand to hand and have a card selected. For explanation's sake, we will use the King of Clubs as our selection.

"Watch as I demonstrate. Please select a card. The King of Clubs. That will be our target card."

You will be controlling the selected card to the second position from the top of the deck, directly underneath the face-up Joker. An easy way to do this is to utilize Dai Vernon's Depth Illusion a/k/a *Tilt* (*Tilt* by Marlo, 1963).

To get your Tilt on, square the deck back into left-hand dealer's grip. Your right hand momentarily approaches the deck from above, just enough for your right thumb to lift off the inner end of the top card of the pack about a half of an inch or so. Apply a small amount of pressure between the base of your left thumb and left fingers to both sides of this

fig. 5

top card, as well as the rest of the deck. This will hold the elevated inner end of the top card in this position as well as keep the outer end of this top card locked down in place with the rest of the deck (fig. 5, from behind). If you are proficient with a one-hand get-ready for Tilt, certainly feel free to "one hand" that bad boy.

Insert the King of Clubs face down into the gap at the inner end of the deck. Due to the depth illusion, from the front, it will look to the spectator as if the card were inserted directly into the center of the pack. Hold a left-pinky break beneath the King and the Joker as you allow the gap to close back down with the rest of the pack. Usually, my preferred clean-up to the move is to use the pinky to push up the bottom fifty cards to meet with the top two, instead of letting the top two cards fall back down to the deck. That does present a better illusion. But since the pinky is busy holding the break, it's all right to relieve him of this extra duty.

"Let's lose it back into the pack somewhere. Nobody knows where the target lies. A random occurrence, one through fifty-two."

From above, lift off the two cards above the break in right-hand Biddle Grip, miscalling them as a "single" ninja card.

"Skill set number one of a ninja is the ability to attack with quick and lethal accuracy. Keep your eye on the ninja card."

fig. 6

Place the remainder of the deck onto the table directly in front of you and then re-adjust your left hand so that it is in position to pick up the top half of the deck in left-hand Biddle Grip. After a "3-2-1" countdown, lift up the top half of the deck an inch or so, and throw the card(s) from your right hand onto the tabled, bottom, half deck. Immediately drop the left-hand cards back onto the pack, trapping the Joker and the hidden selection in between the halves (fig. 6).

"3, 2, 1. There, I think I got it."

Square up the cards with your right hand and place them into left-hand dealer's grip.

"Let's take a look and see if I still got it."

Spread the cards between your hands and stop after you get to the Joker. Break the spread at this point, so that the Joker is the bottom card of the right-hand spread. Allow the spread cards in the left hand to close into dealer's grip and then push the top card of this bottom half over to the right with your left thumb. Flip this top card face up with the edge of the Joker, revealing the selected King.

> *"There it is, The King of Clubs. I guess I do still got it."*

PHASE TWO (MASTER OF DISGUISE)

Lay the Joker face up onto the table and then place the right-hand cards below the ones in the left. Use the opportunity of squaring up the deck into the left hand to catch a pinky break underneath the top two cards of the deck: the face-up King and a face-down "X" card. In this case, the "X" card will be the Ace of Diamonds, which is so obviously the "x-iest" of all the cards in the deck.

Use your right thumb to lift up the inner end of the cards above the break in preparation to perform "Tilt" again. Once the cards are propped into the correct position, use your right middle finger to slide the King toward you until your thumb can contact the card's back. Turn the King face down and slip it into the break beneath the top card, just as before. Continue to hold a pinky break beneath the top card as you pick up the Joker with your right hand.

> *"Let's go ahead and put it back into the pack as we go over ninja skill set number two, becoming a master of disguise."*

fig. 7   fig. 8

Place the face-up Joker on top of the pack, so now you are holding a two-card break.

> *"He can't blend into the crowd very well dressed like this. He'd stand out like a ninja in a deck of cards."*

Pick up the two cards above the break by their opposite corners, your right thumb on the inner right corner and your right middle finger on the outer left corner (fig. 7).

> *"But if we give him a shake..."*

You will be changing the Joker into the "X" card, in our case the Ace of Diamonds, by utilizing Marlo's "In Lieu Of Vernon's Through The Fist Move" a/k/a the Twirl Change (*At The Table* by John Racherbaumer, 1984). The change is executed by allowing your right index finger to extend so that it can reach the far left edge of the cards. If you apply a bit of downward pressure between your thumb and middle finger, you will cause the card(s) to bow just enough to allow your right first finger to extend over and under the left-hand side of the cards. By pulling this side up with the index finger, the card(s) will rotate 180 degrees on the axis of the thumb and middle finger, turning into our "X" card, the Ace of Diamonds (fig. 8).

In order to disguise this twirling action, give the card(s) a few downward shakes as you do the move. The smaller action of "the twirl" is covered by the larger action of "the shakes". As you do the Twirl Change with your

fig. 9

fig. 10

right hand, use your left thumb to push over the top card of the deck, the King, catching a pinky break beneath it. The Twirl Change provides more than enough cover to hide this left-hand action.

"...he dons a clever disguise, making him able to get close enough for a sneak attack..."

Lower the right-hand cards, still in Twirl Change position, back onto the deck, in order to add the card above the break to them. Immediately pick up all three cards above the break and then drop the deck back onto the tabletop. An awesome bonus is that because the right middle finger goes across the front of the cards during the move, it obscures the three-card thickness.

Repeat the entire "lift, throw, drop" actions as before. As soon as the card(s) get trapped between the halves of the deck, square up everything nice and neat.

"... like this."

Place the deck into left-hand dealing position and then spread the cards between your hands until you reach the face-up "X" card, The Ace of Diamonds. Break the spread so that the Ace is on top of the left-hand cards. Use your left thumb to pull the Ace and the face-down Joker beneath it back flush with the deck, but catch a pinky break beneath both of them as they square with the pack. While still holding the spread cards in the right hand, use your right fingertips to grab ahold of the two cards above the break (fig. 9, from below). Use this double to flip over the top card of the left-hand cards, revealing the King yet again.

"Once again, he hits the target dead on. The King of Clubs."

Thumb the King off onto the table and then turn the left-hand cards face up end for end by simply turning your left hand palm down, as your left thumb grabs ahold of the "X" card and face-down Joker below it (fig. 10).

Turn your left hand palm up as you square the double with the rest of the cards and then immediately thumb over the Joker as the right hand makes a magic wave with its spread cards.

PHASE THREE (INVISIBILITY)

Place the right-hand cards below the cards in the left hand and then square up everything into left-hand dealer's grip.

Pick up the King and perform one more false insertion into the deck, but this time, you will not be using Tilt. Instead, approach the back of the deck with the King, but this time, slide it straight to the very bottom of the pack, underneath everything. The spectator has been conditioned by now that every time the card is inserted into the rear of the pack, it is going into "the middle".

Transfer the deck to left-hand dealer's grip, with the index finger now wrapped around the front of the deck, not along the side of the deck with the rest of the fingers. Turn your hand so that the cards are held horizontally with the Joker facing the spectator.

It's time to make the ninja card turn invisible. To do so, you are going to use what is, in my opinion, one of the very best color changes out there: "The Cardini Snap Color Change" from *Card Manipulations 3* (Jean Hugard, 1934). It was discussed briefly in the description for "The Trashcan Production", but in that instance, a card makes an appearance. We will be using it to make the card disappear or turn "invisible".

fig. 11   fig. 12

> *"My favorite of the ninja skills is the ability to actually become invisible. Yes, invisible."*

To perform this absolutely glorious move, the right hand moves over in front of the bottom half of the face-up Joker, with the back of the hand facing the spectator. Flick the center of the Joker with your right index finger while continuing to allow the rest of the hand to do its important job of covering the bottom half of the card.

> *"With a flick, just like that..."*

As soon as you've done the flicking, the left middle finger and pinky quickly pull the Joker's right edge down over the edge of the deck, levering it up into a vertical position. The left ring finger is not involved in the pulling action, but it does act as a wall, stopping the card in its tracks. Because the right hand stayed in its extended position, the Joker is now completely hidden from view from the spectator (fig. 11, exposed side view). For all intents and purposes, the card just instantly "turned invisible".

> *"...he pops out of sight..."*

The last part of this move is the clean-up. Grab the bottom half of the deck between your right thumb and middle finger, while still covering the propped-up Joker. Simply lift the deck up an inch or so, using the left thumb as a pivot point, and then pull the Joker around to the face of the deck with the left fingers (fig. 12). As the card rolls around in line with the rest of the deck, give the cards an upward riffle with the right fingers to "lock" everything in place.

> *"...ready for his final stealth attack. This one really is outta sight because you are going to do the dirty work. Trust us. He's a professional ninja. I...am just an amateur."*

Pretend to hand the spectator the invisible card and instruct them to "practice" throwing it back and forth with you. There is plenty of room for some invisible shenanigans here—the classic "Tossed Too High Over Your Head" goof, or maybe the old "Invisible Paper Cut From Hell" chestnut, or perhaps the ever so funny "Invisible Card Impaled Through the Chest" bit. Kids love that!! Use your imagination.

> *"Take this invisible ninja card and practice throwing it to me, but be careful. This isn't kid's stuff. You could put out an invisible eye with that thing!"*

fig. 13

fig. 14

fig. 15

fig. 16

After a few mimed tosses back and forth, spread the cards between your hands, showing the "middle", but also showing that everything is on the up and up and there are no face-up Jokers hiding out, for those lovely few out there that may be looking.

> *"I'm going to cut the cards down to the table, and when I count down from three, you chuck that baby right into the middle . of the pack, got it?"*

As you close the spread back into left-hand dealer's grip, grab a left pinky break above the bottom card of the deck, the Joker.

SLAP TRAP

"Slap Trap" is an awesome card production in which a card magically appears face up, sticking out of the middle of the deck. It can be used as a single-card revelation or as a multiple one. Perhaps as the final production in your 217th Four-Ace Production routine? Anyway, the manner in which it makes its appearance fits perfectly as the closer to this routine, because as you will see after going over it, it really does give an excellent illusion of a card visibly appearing, as if were just thrown by the spectator.

On the count on "one", the right hand reaches over from above and cuts off about a third of the cards and slaps them onto the table.

> *"One..."*

On the count of "two", the right hand reaches over and again, cuts off another third, and slaps it onto the tabled cards (fig. 13).

> *"Two..."*

Finally, on the count of "three", the right hand cuts all of the cards above the break, as the left hand rolls slightly, but sharply at the wrist, clockwise (fig. 14). This will cause the Joker to roll off the left fingertips, revolving face up as it hangs for a second in the air (fig. 15). The card is not thrown in any way. Just allow the card to do its gravity thing and it will flip over as long as you roll the wrist sharply enough.

"Three!! Do it!!"

As the cards in the right hand are getting ready to get smacked down to the table, they trap the free-floating, face-up Joker in the process and slap it down onto the tabled cards (fig. 16). Put some acting into it and follow the quick flight of the card with your eyes just before it makes its appearance. A little bit of timing on your part, combined with the spectator's pantomime involvement/misdirection, makes this an incredibly visual and fun production.

"Oh yes!! Look at that!! Nice shot. Let's take a look."

Reach over to the deck with your right hand and cut to the face-up Joker. Dramatically lift up the cards to reveal the King of Clubs on the bottom of the top half.

"Very nice shot!!"

Table the top half face up and use both hands to remove the Joker. Stand it up on its end on top of the bottom half of the pack and then use both hands to make the ninja "bow", by simply bending the top half of the card forward.

"From one ninja to another, we bow. The Wannabe Ninja strikes again!!!"

Oh Yeah....

Well, what can I say? This one really is my baby. Hopefully it will be your baby, too. There is a lot of strong magic going on during this routine. The audience participation makes this a treat to perform. Have some fun with various Kung-Fu sound effects and "hiyah"s as the cards are thrown. I have used both of the original productions, Slap Trap and the Trashcan Production, for many, many years. Both are staples in my regular work. For what it is worth, I often perform the Trashcan Production without using a fan as a cover. It is possible to do it with just your outstretched hand, but that is another lesson for another time, grasshopper.

I hope you carry on the ways of the Wannabe Ninja. Learn this routine and you will have a very dynamic piece of routined ninja magic that the audience will really get a "kick" out of. A very special "Wannabe" thank you goes out to two of the magic dojo's greatest publishing sensei, Richard Kaufman and Stephen Minch, for helping track down the appropriate historical references on this one. I was completely ready to give total credit to Bruce Lee and Chuck Norris until Richard and Stephen showed me the light.

Effect

A borrowed key is bent with the "power of the mind". It is then snapped into two pieces, right in front of the spectator's eyes. Holding a piece in either hand, they are chucked toward each other, where they visibly fuse back together good as new.

Needed

A small, two-inch piece of a key (fig. 1). Grab a set of wire cutters and simply just start cutting and bending it back and forth until you can actually snap the needed piece right off from the head of the key. It will take a little bit of effort, but it is really not that difficult to accomplish. Of course, if you have access to some sort of metal cutter that will do the job, then by all means cut away.

Preparation

Begin with the small piece of key pinched between your right thumb and first finger. It should be completely hidden from view. Keep the severed edge of the piece closest to the tips of the fingers (fig. 2). You can get into this position very easily in a pocket, or under a table if seated.

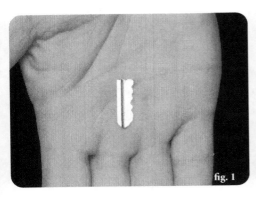
fig. 1

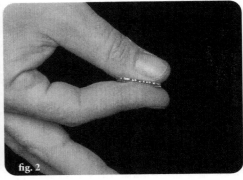
fig. 2

Performance

Borrow a key that somewhat matches the piece you have concealed. A generic house key tends to be the best. Take the key from the spectator with your left hand and transfer it into your pinched right fingers. The tip of the real key should be underneath and perpendicular to the concealed piece being pinched (fig. 3). This is a very clean and open display.

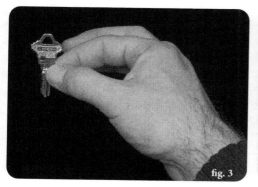

"Do you have a house key I can use for a second? Great. Now, how about the house? Actually, the key will be enough. I promise to return it to you completely unharmed. This is my attempt—and I use the word 'attempt' very loosely—at being one of those wacky, metal-bending, mentalist types. It's not really my cup of tea. I'm more of magic kind of guy. I'd rather bend your mind than your metal."

Using your free left hand, grab ahold of the head of the key and rotate it counter-clockwise, until the tip of the key roughly lines up with the concealed piece. Hold your left hand in an open-grip position, with the fingers pointing upward and the back of the hand facing the spectator. Turn your right hand palm down and place the key, with the concealed piece now on top of it, into your left fingertips. The fingertips of the left hand should only be holding the edges of the metal part of the key, not the head. Using your right index finger, slide the hidden piece down until it is just about even with the end of the real key. The hidden piece should overhang the end of the real key by only a fraction of an inch, enough to make it easy to pick up later on (fig. 4).

Slide the key and the hidden piece as one unit to the right. Do this until the severed edge of the hidden piece is just to the right of the left edge of the first finger. These pieces will be concealed from view by your left fingers. The head of the key will be sticking out to the right side of these fingers.

> *"If I were to do that kind of thing, I suppose it would look something like this. Watch out. This might get a little weird."*

While keeping the entire unit in place with your left fingers and thumb, pinch the concealed piece from above with your right thumb and index finger. The tip of the right thumb should be resting on the pointed end of the hidden piece while the right index finger is on the concealed piece's severed edge (fig. 5).

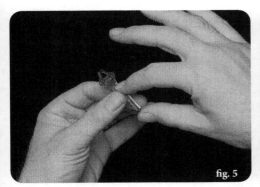
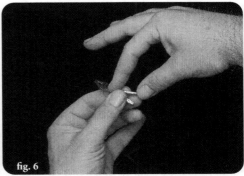

fig. 5   fig. 6

To make the key appear to bend, "tickle" the severed edge of the concealed piece with the right index finger. While you are doing this, the right thumb lifts the hidden piece's end off of the real key. This is easy to do thanks to the overhang. Allow the left thumb and first finger to act as a pivot point (fig. 6, from below). The fingers are actually shown here to be a bit lower and open than they would be in performance. This is solely for purposes of explanation, so do keep those left fingers up in position to screen the lower end of the real key. Also, this bend should be performed slowly and smoothly.

> *"A little bit of heat is all we need. And a bit more, and a bit more, and just a bit more..."*

You are going to give the spectator another angle to view the bent key. Approach the key from behind with your right hand. Clip the concealed end of the real key between your index and middle fingers of the right hand. Allow your right thumb and index finger to pinch the "bent" extra piece in place (fig. 7). Let go of the key with your left hand, holding it in position solely with the right hand. Rotate the back of your right hand so that it faces the spectator and then roll your right hand downward so the back of it is now facing the floor (fig. 8). This entire hand-rotation sequence should be done smoothly, but briskly. There is a tendency to flash the tip of the real key that is sticking out from under the right hand. Keep the right hand rolled forward as much as possible to help alleviate this.

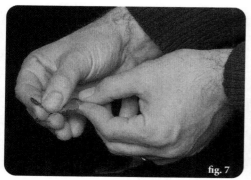

fig. 7   fig. 8

"Looks real, doesn't it? My opinion is this, though: Why bend something when you can just break it?"

Grab the projecting "bent" piece with your left fingertips. While keeping the severed end concealed under the right thumb, the left fingers turn the piece counter-clockwise to the left. It should be at approximately 3:00, but 3:05 would be acceptable...I suppose (fig. 9).

While continuing to keep the severed end trapped under the thumb, use your left fingers to twist this "bent" piece over one full revolution away from you. Then, with a sharp action, pull the piece all of the way off of the metal on the real key. You will get a great scraping sound that sounds like the key just broke into two. The spectator will see two separate pieces (fig. 10).

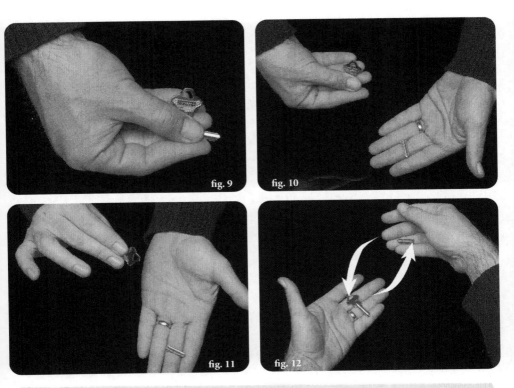

fig. 9   fig. 10   fig. 11   fig. 12

"Ouch. That's gonna leave a mark!!!"

As you show the broken piece in the left hand, allow the right thumb to go under the head of the key. The key is now gripped in place between your right thumb and index finger. Swing the other three fingers up and over the bottom end of the key, so only the head of it is visible. This is covered by the larger action of raising this "half" key up in front of you (fig. 11).

You are in position to visibly restore the key by utilizing Jay Sankey's Two-Way Toss (*100% Sankey* by Richard Kaufman, 1990). This move is a fantastically-funky combination of Ken Krenzel's The Marionette Multiple Coin Vanish (*Apocalypse, Vol. 1-5* by Harry Lorayne, 2000) and David Williamson's Striking Vanish (*Williamson's Wonders* by Richard Kaufman, 1989). To perform the Two-Way Toss, hold your hands approximately six to eight inches apart from one another, with the right hand held about three inches higher than the left. The right hand moves in to about three to four inches from the left hand and tosses its piece directly at the spot occupied by the severed piece. The instant the right-hand piece is released, both hands move slightly, but sharply, down and to the right, ending with an abrupt stop. This will propel the left-hand piece into the loosely opened right fist (fig. 12). There should be no movement from the right hand as it makes the catch. It is a small piece that is being caught, but don't let that psych you out. Just allow the piece to land wherever it does in the right hand, without any re-adjustments. If performed correctly, it will look exactly as if the two pieces of key fuse together on the outstretched left hand.

"That's why I never really went for this type of trick. I mean, if someone is nice enough to lend you their car key, and then I break it into two for entertainment purposes, which I am sure you found extremely entertaining, the least I can do is...put it back together."

Hold the restored key up for everybody to see.

"That is, if I even did that type of mentalist metal-bending 'sham-a-lama-ding-dong' type of thing. But I said before, I just 'sham-a-lama-ding' don't do it. But I'll still take the house if you change your mind."

Hand the key back to the spectator and discreetly ditch the half-key piece when the moment is right.

Oh Yeah….

This is a very visual way to do a classic key-bending trick. I have always shied away from doing a standard key bend because it usually ends up with a genuine bent key. Try borrowing one and doing that to it. I don't think you'll make it out of the room in one piece. Make sure that the spectator is comfortable with you as a person before pretending to damage their key. They should be well aware that you make miracles happen. That will soften the initial blow when they see their key getting bent and broken. This effect is similar in handling to Dr. Sawa's "Gary Uller" spoon-bending-breaking-restoring trick, published in the January 1977 edition of *Genii* Magazine. Now, go get bent!!

twenty

John Guastaferro

Effect

The magician (that's you) states that "TWENTY feels lucky today", so much, in fact, that he places a twenty-dollar bill onto the table along with a single, face-down, lucky card. This $20 is riding on the spectator's ability to win at both blackjack and poker by using nothing more than the magician's most excellent good luck. The deck is thoroughly shuffled by the audience (cut, mixed, riffle-shuffled, etc.).

First up, blackjack. The magician guarantees the spectator will end up with an almost sure-fire, winning hand of "TWENTY", with no chance of busting whatsoever. Knowing this, the spectator keeps hitting their original two-card hand until, sure enough, five cards have been dealt, totaling "TWENTY". To top it off, that lucky card that was placed next to the bill turns out to be an Ace, bringing the hand to a winning twenty-one. How very lucky.

Poker time. The spectator is now instructed to gather up the cards previously dealt and to try and form the best poker hand possible with them. No pairs or flushes are to be found, but as the magician's good luck would have it, there is a straight—another winning hand for the spectator! And just because we magicians are in the business of blowing minds, the "TWENTY"-dollar bill is turned over to show the prediction "STRAIGHT" written in big, bold letters across its face!

Needed

A deck of your favorite playing cards, a twenty-dollar bill, and a permanent marker.

Preparation

Using the marker, write the word "STRAIGHT" on one side of the twenty and then put this bill into your pocket (fig. 1).

I write it on the face because I like the imagery that creates when the writing goes over the president's face. John writes it down across the back of the bill. It's these little differences in life that make us all truly unique and special, right?

Now, go through the deck and remove two sets of the following cards: a Two, a Three, a Four, a Five, and a Six. In the poker world, this five-card combination is known as a straight. If you do not know this already, we should definitely play poker some time soon. You can use any suit; in fact, it's probably best to have a nice mix of suits within your two straights, as it will look better in the end.

Place one of these straights on top of the face-down deck in any order. Next, place the other straight face down on top of the deck, in the same order as the first one. In our example, the first straight is running in the following order: Two, Four, Five, Three, and Six. The second straight is then placed on top of the first, in Two, Four, Five, Three, Six order as well (fig. 2).

Lastly, place an Ace face down on top of everything and you are set.

fig. 1   fig. 2

Performance

OK, it's show time. You need to keep the two straights and the Ace on top of the deck as you go ahead and execute your favorite sequence of false cuts, as flashy and self-indulgent as you can muster up. Now, normally, I'm not one for the overuse of flourishes or all the super-snazzy deck-cutting procedures that all the kiddos are doing these days (probably because I simply cannot do the vast majority of them), but on this occasion, it makes perfect sense to engage in a little show-off session with the deck, as it justifies the reason that somebody would want to use your "amazing" card skills in a gambling situation. Plus, since the majority of this routine is performed outside of the magician's skillful hands, this is your time to shine like a champ, so go for it. Eye of the tiger!

"When people see me do my thing with playing cards, they often say, 'Man, I should take you to Vegas.' Just so you know, if you're buyin', I'm flyin'!"

Bring your glorious false-cutting sequence to a close and then take the top card off of the deck (the Ace) and table it face down directly in front of you.

"But we won't be using any magic. We will use luck. Here, this is going to be a 'lucky card', if we should need it…but something tells me we won't need it all."

Place the deck face down, right next to this "lucky card".

"You see, you may not know this about me, but I am officially the luckiest person on the face of the earth, and not just because I'm lucky enough to be here with you right now."

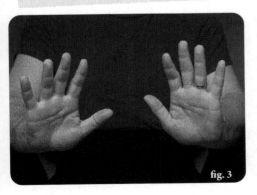
fig. 3

After you've sufficiently sucked-up to your audience, continue on explaining your good luck to them. When you say the word "twenty", hold out both hands in front of you with all ten fingers extended, which, of course, is the universal sign for "ten" (fig. 3). Fold your fingers inward and then extend them back open into another display of "ten". You math wizards out there will recognize this double flashing of "ten" as a way to convey the number "twenty". Those that don't recognize this will just have to take my word for it.

> *"It's truly as if I can't lose. I have a feel for it, and right now, I'm definitely feeling 'twenty'."*

Look the spectator in the eye, and ask quizzically:

> *"Your birthday is not on the twentieth, is it?"*

Wait for the spectator to answer your question, which will most likely be a "no". In the event that your spectator was actually born on the twentieth, milk this tremendous moment for everything it's worth because, frankly, things like that just don't happen often enough in life.

After they have given their answer, ponder it for a brief moment, saying:

> *"No? Well right now, I'd bet the farm on the number twenty... if you have a farm, that is."*

Suddenly act as if you have just figured out a way to test your lucky "twenty" theory.

> *"You know, I have an idea. Let's test it out. If we were in Vegas, we could do a few different things. Maybe we could play roulette and put it all on the number twenty. Would you happen to have a small roulette table on you, per chance?"*

After the spectator answers your ridiculous question, pick up the deck of cards and spread them between your hands.

> *"No? Well I suppose we could demonstrate it with some of the card games then. Maybe blackjack and poker? Those are pretty popular games."*

Square up the deck and then reach into your pocket and take out the twenty-dollar bill. Table it next to the "lucky card", writing side down, as you propose your test of luck.

> *"In fact, I am so confident in my ability to bring you the winning luck that you deserve, I am willing to wager twenty dollars of my hard-earned magic money that when put to the test, you will win at both a hand of blackjack and of poker. Are you in? Awesome. This will be fun."*

While it is possible to have the spectator deal the cards to themselves, I strongly believe that a second spectator should join in on the festivities. Along with possessing basic card-shuffling abilities, select somebody who also projects "safety and sweetness" in their persona. While I love to root against the dealer in almost all scenarios, we certainly do not want the second spectator feeling as if the rest of the audience is pitted up against them. All three of you are in this experiment together, not two against one, or even worse, the entire audience against one.

> *"First off, we need someone else to come up here and to act as our dealer. I don't want to do it. I'm just here for the good luck."*

Bring your second spectator up to the performing area and situate yourself so that you are in between your two helpers.

> *"OK, excellent. I assume you can shuffle and mix cards. Great! Let's start off and make sure that all of the cards are mixed."*

Holding the deck in left-hand dealer's grip, extend it toward the first spectator and ask them to cut off about a third of the pack. Remember that your setup (the two straights) is on top of this portion of the deck, so make sure that the first spectator cuts off more than those top ten cards. If they did not, gently scold them for their terrible estimation skills and then ask them to replace the cards back onto the deck and then to repeat the cutting procedure so that the stack on top stays intact.

"Here, cut off about a third of these."

Turn toward the second spectator (the dealer) and have them cut off about half of the remaining cards (another third).

"Now, will you please do the same?"

To further display a sense of randomness, ask the spectators to now switch their packets with each other. The second spectator now has the portion of the deck with the stack on top of it.

"Great. Now, you two switch packets with each other..."

Finally, trade your cards with the second spectator (the dealer). Again, under the guise of randomizing the mixing procedure, you know have the portion of the deck with the secret stack on top of it.

"...and now you switch with me."

fig. 4

You will be leading your two spectators through a brief face-down mixing of the cards in their hands. To the spectators, it will simply look as if you are mixing up the cards, and that is exactly what they will be doing when following your actions. While the spectators' cards will be

fig. 5

fig. 6

genuinely mixed, your cards will not, as you will be utilizing a terrific in-the-hands false shuffle entitled the Charlier Shuffle (*The Royal Road To Card Magic* by Jean Hugard and Fred Braue, 1948). This shuffle is extremely deceiving, yet completely easy to do. It will appear as if the cards are being hopelessly mixed, when in reality, nothing more than a series of straight cuts is being performed.

While holding the pack in left-hand dealer's grip, use your left thumb to push over about five cards into the right hand. These cards will be gripped between the right thumb and fingers, with the fingers contacting the cards' faces (fig. 4). Next, with the left fingers, push over five cards or so from the bottom of the left-hand cards. Take these on top of the cards in your right hand, readjusting the right thumb so that it can clamp down on top of everything in order to hold them in place (fig. 5). Again, using your left thumb, push off yet another small batch of cards from the top of the pack, taking them underneath the cards in the right hand (fig. 6). Repeat this alternating "on top/underneath" cutting pattern until all of the cards are now in your right hand. Do not let the ease of this shuffle turn you off. For my money, it's the best "in-the-hands" false shuffle out there.

"Excellent. Go ahead and mix up your cards like this. You will often see dealers mixing the cards like this on the blackjack table before the game starts."

After completing your individual "shuffles", instruct the spectators to turn their cards face up, as you do the same. It appears as if you are simply showing that the cards are genuinely

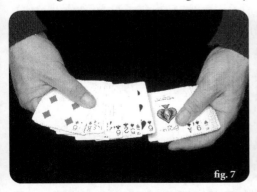

fig. 7

fig. 8

mixed, but what you are really going to do is spread your cards with the faces slightly angled toward yourself as you look for the card that was originally on top of the deck (the top card of your secret stack). Separate the spread so that this original top card is now on the bottom of the face-up cards in the right hand (fig. 7). Cut these right-hand cards underneath the cards in the left hand. The complete stack is now on the bottom of your face-up cards. Drop your cards face up onto the table and then instruct one of the spectators to drop their cards face up on top of yours.

"If you take a quick look at the cards, you can see that there is no doubt at all that they are mixed. Here, drop yours on top of mine..."

Ask the other spectator to drop their cards face up on top of everything.

"...and will you please do the same?"

Now, pick up the face-up deck from above in right-hand Biddle grip and use your right index finger to swing cut the top half into left-hand dealer's grip. The stack is on the bottom of the right-hand half. Rotate both halves of the deck so that they are each being held in a vertical position, with the right hand held slightly higher than the left (fig. 8). As you are now in

perfect overhand shuffle position, use your left thumb to singly run the top five cards from the right half onto the top of the cards in the left hand. If you were to check the status of the cards, you would see that the top five cards of each face-down half now each have a straight on top of it, the only difference being that each of the straights are now running in

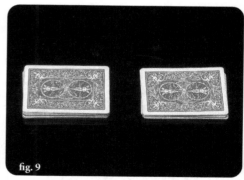

fig. 9

opposite directions (or mirror images) of each other.

After stopping your overhand shuffle after the top five cards have been run, "realize" that the second spectator should actually be the one shuffling the cards, not you. Throw the cards from the right hand on top of the left, holding a left pinky break between the two halves.

> *"But actually, let's have our dealer do their job and give the deck one more thorough mix."*

Cut the cards above the pinky break to the table and then place the lower half of the deck right next to them, ends facing each other, in preparation for a riffle shuffle (fig. 9).

> *"Are you up for the task? The outcome is going to be completely dependent upon your professional shuffle...of course, no pressure."*

Now, we are going to jump into the wild and wonderful world of the Gilbreath Principle (*The Linking Ring*, Vol. 38, no. 5, 1958), a piece of utter amazement discovered by Norman Gilbreath that outlines the fact that when a specific sequence of cards is riffle shuffled into another packet consisting of the reverse order of the same specific sequence, certain incredible outcomes will mathematically occur, every time, all of the time. Now, we are not going to delve into the inner workings of this mind-boggling principle, as there are plenty of other resources out there that explain it in detail. You could spend a lifetime trying to get inside of why or how this principle works. For now, just know that it does work and that's good enough for me.

We are in a perfect position for this principle, since the top five cards of each half are, indeed, in reverse order of each other. Instruct the dealer to shuffle those two halves together and to square up the cards.

> *"Do it like you see in a casino and give those cards a real-life, honest-to-God riffle shuffle and then push them together, nice and neat."*

After the spectator shuffles the halves together, pick up the deck and hand it to the dealer.

> *"Wow! You are good...but hopefully we will be just a little bit better."*

Here is where your world is going to get weird in a "Gilbreath" kind of way. I am here to tell you that even though the deck was honestly riffle shuffled by the spectator/dealer, the top five cards of the deck will now absolutely and unequivocally be a Two through Six straight, in no particular order or suit arrangement. Go ahead and check. There will be a Two, a Three, a Four, a Five, and a Six. Incredible! The mathematical properties of the Gilbreath Principle guarantee that will happen every single time. And what's even better? When you add the Two through Six together, what number do you think comes up? That's right. They all add up to the number twenty! Double incredible! Now let's have some fun with this principle.

"OK, here we go."

Instruct the dealer to deal two cards face down. Now, I know that in regulation games of blackjack, the cards are dealt face up, but in this instance, we will deal all of the cards face down, until the final fifth card. I believe that most spectators would not see the straight appear if the cards were being dealt face up because they would be concentrating solely on what numbers they need to get to twenty. But as extra insurance, I think it's a good idea to keep them face down.

"First, blackjack. Go ahead and deal two cards face down."

Instruct the spectator to look at the faces of the two cards just dealt. We will assume in this instance the spectator received a Three and a Six, totaling nine.

"Go ahead and look at your hand. Now, I keep seeing 'twenty' flash in front of my eyes. Did you get twenty? No? Don't worry. You will, I promise. Just keep hitting, OK?"

Instruct the dealer to deal another card face down to the spectator.

"Go ahead and deal another card face down so we can add that to the hand."

Give the spectator a second to look at the new face-down card and then to add it to their hand. Again, in this example, a Four is our next card, bringing the current total to thirteen.

"How about now? No?"

Instruct the dealer to deal off another face-down card for the spectator to pick up, look at, and add to their total of thirteen. We will assume that this fourth card is a Two, bringing the hand to a very losable fifteen.
Ask the spectator if this fourth card has given them a total of twenty, to which they will reply that it hasn't. You will now find out exactly what card is needed to reach our lucky twenty.

"Twenty yet? No? Well, what card do you need in order to get a twenty?"

Depending on which card the spectator needs, you now have an opportunity to include a funny little bit. If they report that they need a Four, Five, or a Six, well, that would imply that they have a bad hand of fourteen, fifteen, or sixteen. All three of those are hands in which one would naturally want to hit to improve their chance of winning. If that is the case, come to grips with the fact that there will be no "bonus joke" for you right now and then proceed to give the instructions to the dealer to deal the last card face up. If they should state that they need a Two or a Three, then that implies that they are hitting on a seventeen or an eighteen. Those are both "highly bustable" hands that one would probably never want to hit on. So, if this is what happens and they say a "Two", for example, do a comedic double take and act completely surprised by their terrible card sense.

fig. 10

> *"A Two? And you want to hit? Are you sure? What kind of maniac hits on an eighteen? The answer? My kind of maniac."*

After that statement of reassurance, ask the dealer to deal that last card face up. This is a really fun moment in the routine, and I have to admit that when performing it, I do secretly wish that it would turn out this way every time. The good news is that it does happen quite a lot. But, since not everything turns out the way we always want it to, let's just assume for explanation purposes that the spectator identifies that they need a four to hit that magic number of twenty. No "bonus joke" this time, but there is plenty of amazement coming to keep everybody entertained.

> *"A Four? Well, go ahead and give her one more card, but this time, deal it face up (fig. 10)."*

After the Four has been dealt face up, burst into applause and celebration.

> *"A Four! Yes! What did I tell you?*
> *With your natural charm and my natural luck, we can't lose."*

With your index finger, count each one of the five cards to show to everyone the total number of cards it took to hit twenty.

> *"And look at this: you have a twenty with five cards. Actually, they call that a 'Five-Card Charlie'. That's a '1-in-50' chance! Not too shabby."*

Point to the lucky card that you tabled earlier and then push it toward the spectator with instructions to turn it over.

> *"Oh yeah, remember that lucky card? I really didn't think we'd need it, but just for kicks, turn it over and see if it would have helped your hand at all."*

After the spectator turns over the Ace, pick it up, show it around to everyone, and then place it face up next to the five-card hand, making it a six-card twenty-one.

"An Ace!! A perfect hand of twenty-one. By the way, the odds of having a six-card hand that adds up to twenty-one are 1 in 400, which we will naturally call a 'Six-Card Jennifer' (or whatever name you would care to use)."

Pick up the Ace and place it back onto the deck. Feel free to give the cards a shuffle while you talk, if that makes you happy.

"OK. Blackjack is fine for the kids, but poker, well, that is a true test to my luck."

Instruct the spectator to now pick up their five-card hand and to see if any type of decent poker hand can be made out of it.

"Let's see. Take a look at your hand. Can you form any type of decent Poker hand with them? Do you have a pair? Maybe a three of a kind? How about a flush? No? Well, I feel that you have a winning hand anyway."

Look the spectator in the eye in all seriousness and ask if they have received a straight.

"Wait a second. Do you happen to have a straight?"

After the spectator acknowledges that they have, indeed, received a straight, take the cards from the spectator and show the faces all around in absolute astonishment.

"You do? Fantastic!! Another winning hand. I need to point out that the odds of dealing a straight right off of the top of the deck are 1 in 72,000. That…is some serious luck!"

Take the five cards and add them to the deck, before putting it away into your pocket.

"But you know, sometimes luck isn't always enough. In those times, a sure thing is needed, and in this case I knew that you getting a straight was going to be a sure thing."

Pick up the twenty and slowly turn it over to show the predicted word "STRAIGHT" written on the back of the bill.

"That's why I took a one in a million shot and wrote the word 'STRAIGHT' on the back of the twenty-dollar bill before we ever even started."

Oh Yeah....

Ahhh yes. The scary Gilbreath Principle. Well, as you can see, there is nothing scary or overtly mathematical about this application of the principle. This routine is overflowing with commercial appeal. John's inspiration for this routine came from Howard Hamburg's "Hidden Prediction" from his excellent *Sessions* DVD (2011). John says, "The way that the Gilbreath Principle was used to cause seemingly random cards to add to a predetermined total was very fooling." Taking it from a straight-ahead prediction trick to a gambling-themed routine certainly does crank up the commercial appeal way past twenty.

Effect

A "pencil-paper" ink transposition, if you will. A "mean-hearted" permanent marker insultingly writes the word "pencil" on a signed business card, as well as the word "paper" along the side of a pencil. In a magical moment of "self-realization", the ink on the pencil visually morphs into the word "pencil". The signed card also "finds itself" as it's turned over to show that it now says "paper".

Needed

An ordinary yellow No. 2 pencil. These pencils almost always have the required shiny outer-casing that is needed to make this magic happen. You will also need a stack of business cards, a pair of scissors, a rubber band, a permanent fine-tip marker, and finally, a fine-tip dry-erase marker.

Preparation

Set the pencil down in front of you so that the pointed end is facing toward your right. With the permanent marker, write the word "pencil" along the side of the pencil, about an inch or two from the pointed end. The entire word should be no more than an inch or so in length (fig. 1). The writing will fit very nicely inside one of the pencil's hexagonal sides. If your pencil is of the "round" variety and has no sides, well, that sounds like some kind of a personal problem to me. My advice to you: get yourself another pencil. If you are a rebel and must live dangerously, just "eyeball" it.

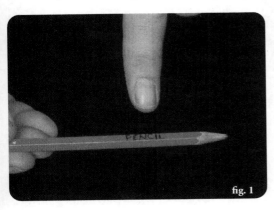

fig. 1

Next, place a tiny dot right under the metal sleeve that holds the eraser, directly opposite of the side that now says "pencil". This indicator dot will help you quickly know where to write the word "paper" later. One last thing: if your pencil has been cursed with one of those big No. 2 marks close to the eraser end (or any other brand-name labels or writing, for that matter), scrape it off with the scissors. It doesn't have to be spotless. You just want as clean of a pencil as you can muster up. Here's a helpful household tip. Get one of those Magic Eraser-type products from your local grocery store. It will do a great job removing that ink.

Lastly, take out a business card and cut it in half with scissors. Discard the left half and set the right half aside. Write the word "paper" on the bottom left corner of one of the other business cards and then place this card on top of the stack (fig. 2). Place the half card directly over the left side of the top card and then wrap the rubber band around the center of the stack, covering the cut edge of the half card (fig. 3). You are going to utilize an amazing principle that goes all the way back to the 17th century, but was popularized for modern magic audiences in 1946 as the marketed item "Out to Lunch" by

fig. 2 fig. 3

Clare Cummings and Bob Ellis.. Place the stack of business cards, the pencil, and the dry-erase marker into your pocket. Get rid of the scissors and the permanent marker and you are ready to go.

Performance
Hold the stack of cards in one hand and the pencil in the other. Be careful to not let the writing on the pencil accidentally flash while you are displaying the items.

"Here's a little quiz for you. A pencil and a piece of paper. What do these two things have in common?"

Place both items onto the table in front of you, again being careful to not expose the writing on the pencil. I find it best to table the stack of cards and then to place the pencil down with the writing facing you. The tip of the pencil should overlap the corner of the cards. This will prevent the pencil from accidentally rolling over and exposing the secret writing.

"It has to do with where they both come from. Here's another hint."

Make a "T" symbol with your hands, like a "time-out", when you say the letter "T".

"It begins with the letter 'T' and they sprout up everywhere. The answer?"

Point with both fingers as you say "Target" and hold that pose for a few awkward beats. After that moment of quasi-weirdness, relax your arms and pick up the business cards in the left hand and the pencil in the right.

"Target.... No, I'm just kidding. The real answer is...trees. Both the pencil and a piece of paper originally come from trees."

You should be holding the pencil between your right thumb and first two fingers, thumb on top. Note that the word "pencil" is on the underside of the pencil, concealed by your index and middle fingers. You are going to show the "normalness" of this pencil by utilizing one Paddle Move. ONE!! For the few out there that are unfamiliar with this move, and I find that pretty amazing, here is the briefest of descriptions. Two things happen simultaneously. The first is that the pencil is rotated half of a

fig. 4

revolution away from you. This is accomplished by essentially smearing the thumb and the first two fingers together. This action causes the pencil to do its "rolling" thing. As the fingers do their "smear-roll" (that's a new word!), your hand rotates from a palm-up position to palm down, which shows a "second" blank side (fig. 4).

This is the same natural action that would occur if you were to really show both sides. This larger action of turning over the hand covers the smaller action of rolling the pencil. The audience only sees one side, but believes that they have seen both. Do not overuse this move. Nobody is chasing you. Showing each side of an item once is the natural action that we are looking to replicate. Repeating it too many times just makes people question why you are working so hard to prove it to them that the pencil has two "normal" sides.

> *"The pencil is a little more organic. It even kinda still looks like a tree branch."*

Pick up the business cards in your left hand and display both sides of the banded stack as you say:

> *"But the paper has been cut, processed, bleached, and printed on. Doesn't really look like a tree at all. But even though they're both proud to 'be a tree', they do have a very strong sense of individuality. And they certainly wouldn't like being called by the wrong name. It's a tree-pride thing."*

Set down both items, just as before, and then bring out the marker. Uncap it and slowly pretend as if you are going to scribble on the spectator. They will naturally pull back, proving your point that the marker is "pretty ruthless", as you explain:

> *"But all of the pride in the world can't save them from this powerful guy. Here comes Mean Mr. Marker, a bully who gets off on insulting everybody. He's pretty ruthless. I know they are just words and all, but his remarks are pretty permanent."*

Use the marker to write the word "pencil" on the bottom right corner of the half card, so that it is in the same location as the writing on the top card directly underneath it.

> *"Watch as the marker viciously calls the piece of paper the dreaded 'P' word. That's right. He just called him 'pencil'. That's probably the biggest insult out there in the processed paper world. Just awful!"*

Next, draw a small circle on the right side of the exposed half of the top card

fig. 5   fig. 6

and have the spectator place their name or initials inside of it (fig. 5). This most excellently puts you in a position where the spectator believes that they have signed a card that reads "pencil", but thanks to the half card, they have actually signed the business card that says "paper". Please take a moment and blow a magical kiss of appreciation to the wonderful "Out to Lunch" principle. Now, turn your left hand palm down and slide out the bottom card (really the top full-length card) from the banded stack and table it face down.

> *"Do me a favor and put your initials on this victimized piece of paper. This shows that you have just witnessed this disgusting display of anti-paper persecution."*

Take the marker back from the spectator with your right hand as your left hand picks up and then holds the pencil from above by the eraser end. Remembering to keep the word "pencil" hidden from view, write the word "paper" on the side of the pencil that contains the little indicator dot (fig. 6).

Again, write this word in the same location and style as the word on the other side.

> *"And if that wasn't bad enough, Mean Mr. Marker turns right around and lobs a four-letter word attack on the pencil, calling him 'paper', which actually has five letters, making it even worse!!!! Ouch!! Sticks and stones can break your bones, but WORDS...cause permanent damage."*

Cap the marker and put it away in your pocket as you say:

> *"Let's just get rid of Mean Mr. Marker altogether, because frankly, he makes me sick!!!"*

Transfer the eraser end of the pencil to your palm-up right hand. Grip it from underneath between your right thumb and first two fingers. Holding the pencil parallel to the floor, bring it up to chest height to display. During this transfer, be very careful not to flash the upside-down word "pencil", which should now be staring you right in the face while the spectator sees the word "paper". Point to the stack of cards and the pencil with your free left hand, as you say:

> *"There, I feel better. Don't you? I can't stand bullies. I mean, look at what he did to these two things. They are pretty mixed up right now. Hurt and suffering. They don't even know who they are right now. But this is where their strong sense of individualism comes in."*

Bring your left hand right up to the pointed end of the pencil, about two to three inches from it.

> *"Watch the pencil. If he believes in who he really is..."*

Two things will now happen simultaneously. Snap your left fingers to create that very special magic moment as your right thumb and first two fingers repeat the smearing action from earlier. This will cause the pencil to rotate half of a revolution away from you, bringing the word "pencil" into view (fig. 7).

fig. 7   fig. 8

"...he starts looking and feeling like a pencil..."

You will now wipe off the dry erase "paper" as you rub your fingers across the newly transformed "pencil", as you naturally show that the ink is "permanent". To do this, simply approach the left side of the pencil from underneath with your left hand. Your left index finger will contact the dry-erase "paper" on your side of the pencil as your left thumb slides across the permanent ink "pencil" (fig. 8). This entire rub away can be done with one swipe to the left. As soon as you have wiped your side of the pencil clean, rotate it around slowly, showing that there are no other ink markings on it.

"...permanently."

Set the pencil down with the word "pencil" facing upright. Pick up the business card and display its back as you say:

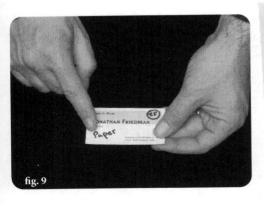

fig. 9

"And the same thing with the paper. Deep down, it knew that it wasn't really a pencil. And even though you witnessed the assault from earlier..."

Slowly turn the business card around and point to the newly transformed "paper" written on it (fig. 9), saying:

> *"...now, it's a bona fide piece of paper again...with your signature still on there and everything."*

Set the card down right next to the pencil for a pretty little display as you pick up the stack of business cards and put them away. You are now super clean. Be sure to give the business card to your spectator, and while you are at it, give someone the pencil, too. That would make you a "star"!!

> *"Even though they are both strong individuals, they do have that mighty tree gene running through them. We all have our Mean Mr. Markers to deal with. Just be yourself, kids. Remember, you can take the pencil and paper out of the tree, but you will never take the tree out of the paper and pencil."*

Oh Yeah….

There is something incredibly satisfying about knowing that the modus operandi for this effect really comes down to two classic principles in magic: the Paddle Move and "Out to Lunch". I seriously considered calling this effect "Out to Lunch…With a Paddle" or even simply "Out to Paddle". Add in the wonders of the dry -erase marker…and you have miracles, man.

I have another unpublished version of the principle that uses only the pencil called "Cheaters Always Win". So, consider it published now. A freebee!! It's based on an effect of David Harkey's called "Crib Sheet" from *Simply Harkey*, 1991. The idea was that you turn a smudge mark on your hand into the "correct answer" while "cheating on a test". In Harkey's extremely rad version, the change of writing took place on the inside of the fingers, which makes sense because if you were planning on cheating and hiding an answer, you could do it on the inside of the fingers. That being said, I couldn't physically get the required mechanics to flow for me, so I came up with the pencil angle. What else would be acceptable to keep out in the open if one was planning on cheating on a test? A pencil. I knew my past devious school ways would finally be put to good use! The handling is virtually the same. Secretly write "E=MC2" or some other "answer" on one side of the pencil. After using the Paddle Move to show both sides blank, draw a smudgy squiggle on the other side of the pencil. The rest is exactly the same. Make the change and clean up the dirty stuff. Richard Sanders has also put out some excellent work involving dry - erase markers and Paddle Moves, so go grab a dry -erase marker and wipe your way into this brave new world.

Coins A La Carte

Atom Split..$100

Up & Over Vanish...........................$1,000

Emerge...$10,000

Arcade Vanish............................$100,000

Denim Ditch.........................$1,000,000

One-Hand Clap...........................Your Soul

Effect

A coin is borrowed and split into two. After the original coin is returned to its rightful owner, the newly split coin goes through a series of mystifying vanishes and appearances.

These are actually six of my original moves that have been strung together to form a routine. Each move can be performed on its own (à la carte), as opposed to being solely a part of the routine.

Needed

Two quarters. One is borrowed from a spectator and the other is yours.

Preparation

None, except easy access to a willing spectator with a quarter to lend. If you do not have a friend with a quarter, get some new friends.

Performance

Begin with a quarter classic palmed in your right hand. Ask a spectator if they have a quarter that you can borrow. Hold the coin by its edges and wiggle it back and forth between the fingertips of both hands, as if you were going to perform the old bending-coin gag. You are about to split their coin into two, with a move called The Atom Split. This move was originally published in *Genii* Magazine's "Magicana" (August 2014). Thank you to Richard Kaufman for allowing me to feature it here as well.

——————— THE ATOM SPLIT ———————

Place the borrowed coin onto your palm-up left hand. This coin should be resting on the tips of your middle and ring fingers. While holding the right hand in a loosely cupped position, release the palmed coin onto fingertip rest position. You are going to secretly load this coin underneath your palm-up left hand. To do so, move your right hand toward your left hand, making sure that as the hands approach each other, only the back of the right hand can be seen by the spectator. The fingers of the left hand are going to enter your cupped right hand, and lay directly on top of the right-hand coin (fig. 1).

While keeping the back of the left-hand fingers in contact with the concealed coin, revolve your right hand clockwise, bringing the hand palm up. This is done the instant you feel the right-hand coin touch the back of your left-hand fingers. Place both thumbs on top of the borrowed coin, as the hidden coin remains concealed directly underneath your left middle and ring fingers, supported in place by your right fingertips (fig. 2).

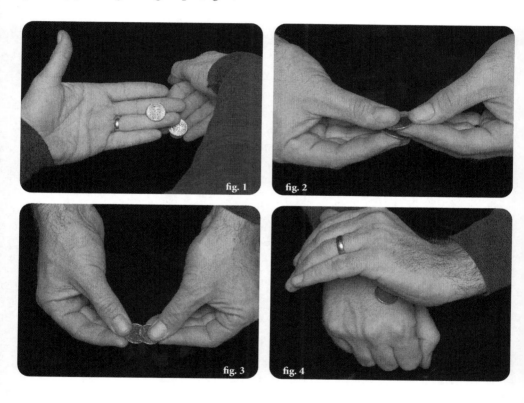

After holding this position for a beat, the right-hand fingertips pull the hidden coin up and to the right, letting it scrape off of the visible coin, which is also being slightly pushed to the right with your left thumb (fig. 3). This will result in a nice, audible, "click" sound.

"I'd like to show you something very interesting with one of your quarters. I bet you didn't know that if you heat up the coin like this, it's completely possible to break it into…two coins. Pretty weird, huh? I don't do this a lot because it really burns my fingers, but hey, that's show biz!"

After handing back the spectator's coin, you place the newly split coin onto the back of your right fist, to "allow it to cool off". It should be a loose fist, held out in front of you.

You are going to vanish this coin using a variation of the L'Homme Masqué coin-loading move (*New Modern Coin Magic* by J. B. Bobo, 1952), but it will be cleverly utilized as a vanish instead of a production. This vanish is entitled the Up and Over Vanish.

THE UP AND OVER VANISH

Beginning with your right elbow bent, so that the thumb hole is facing your body, your left hand approaches the coin resting on the back of your loosely clenched right fist. Let the heel of your left thumb come in direct contact with the coin, as the rest of your fingers start to wrap around your right fist (fig. 4). The heel of your left thumb drags the quarter toward your right thumb hole, as your right hand rotates outward, bringing the thumb hole to face toward the ceiling (fig. 5). Drag the quarter directly into the right-hand thumb hole, as your left hand pretends to grab the coin off of the back of your hand, and moves away to the left, supposedly with the coin (fig. 6). Because both hands are rolling outward slightly as the "take" is happening,

fig. 5

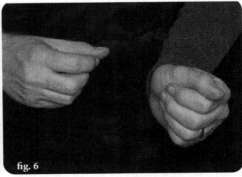

fig. 6

the back of the left hand does a very nice job of obscuring the coin as it drops into the right hand.

Once the coin has fallen into your right hand, let the coin lie in fingertip rest position before pushing it into classic palm. Do this as you show the coin has vanished from the left hand, or in this case, dissolved into small particles.

"Since it's so hot right now, let's just let it sit for a little bit. Watch what happens if we don't give it enough time to properly cool down. And... there it goes. Now, it's broken down into some kind of funky fine powder. This powder is worth A LOT more than twenty-five cents on the street, I'll tell you that much!!"

Pantomime as if you are rolling microscopic particles between your left thumb and index finger. Place these "particles" into your right fingertips, while keeping the back of your right hand facing toward the audience (fig. 7).

In order to make this coin reappear, you will utilize one of my favorite coin productions, Emerge.

EMERGE

Pretend to place these "particles" back onto your palm-up, left-hand fingertips. Just as in The Atom Split, you are going to feed the coin that is in right-hand fingertip rest position directly under your outstretched left

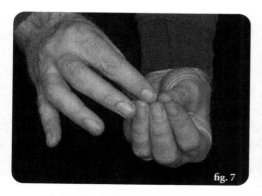
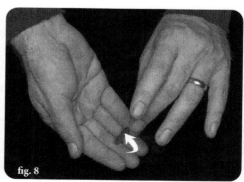

fig. 7   fig. 8

fingertips. With your right thumb tip, pretend to brush the little pieces across the middle and ring fingertips of your left hand.

"I know it's a little hard to see, but if I hold it directly under the light..."

Two things happen at once. Your left thumb, index, and middle fingers make a pinching action as the hand turns face down, miming tossing the pieces into the right hand. While this is happening, the right fingertips close in just enough to cause the coin to flop over one revolution from the right fingertips onto your right palm (fig. 8). It should look like the microscopic pieces visibly meld together as they are tossed from one hand to the other.

"...you can see the coin a little bit better, can't you?"

This highly visual coin appearance can also be performed without the "pinch and throw" move, which is how I usually perform this production. Performed this way, it really does have the appearance of an instant flash appearance of a coin from nowhere.

In order to perform it as such, the handling is exactly the same, except for the "pinch and throw" and the "brushing of the pieces". Instead, the right hand shuttles its coin under the left-hand fingertips, just as before, showing that both hands are empty. Since so much of the open hands are seen, the audience believes that they are truly empty. Hold this position for a second or two and perform the "flop" with the coin. This will propel the coin into view on the right palm. As you do this, your left hand quickly turns face down and makes a magic pass. This pass is really just a tensing of the outstretched left hand (fig. 9). The larger motion of turning the hand over and the magic pass disguise the act of the coin being propelled onto your open right palm. Emerge has some similarities to Giacomo Bertini's beautiful Pinky Transfer move (*The Linking Ring* "One Man Parade", Sept. 2010) in the secret

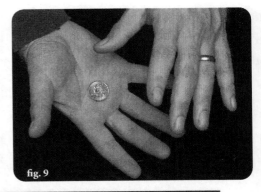

fig. 9

shuttling of the coin under the palm-up left hand. Emerge has a few minor technical differences in finger placements, as the coin is transferred with the tips of both the middle and ring fingers. Emerge really differentiates itself due to the "flash" nature of the production, whereas in Bertini's awesome move, the coin mysteriously appears inside of the closed fist. This does not make my independently created move better. It just presents a different way to take your magic.

This next vanish is something that I came up with back when I was a wee lad. I was hanging around at the arcade (remember those?) when I invented this nifty little coin disappearance. Because of that, I call it The Arcade Vanish, which was originally published in January 2015 edition of *Genii* Magazine's "Magicana". Again, thanks so much to Richard Kaufman for allowing me to feature it here as well.

THE ARCADE VANISH

Pick up the coin and hold it in your right hand, thumb below and your first two fingers above. Make a loose fist with your left hand and hold it out on front of you, with the thumb hole tilting toward your face. You are going to make it appear as if you place the coin directly into your left fist, but what you really do is allow the coin to contact the edge of your curled-in left first finger (fig. 10). The coin is going to get pushed up the length of the inside of your right thumb, into thumb-palm position, as your right thumb pokes into your left thumb hole. The mechanics of this vanish are similar to that of a sponge ball vanish. The very act of "placing" the coin into your left fist

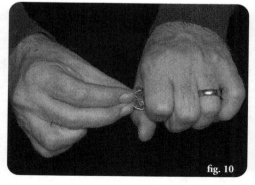
fig. 10

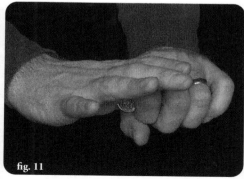
fig. 11

actually puts the coin into thumb palm for you (fig. 11). Two maneuvers for the price of one.

> *"And if I squeeze the coin as hard as I can, the heat from my sweaty, grubby, little fingers transfers deep into the coin. That should start to break it down again in a few seconds."*

You are going to completely vanish the coin by ditching it into your pocket. I always felt a little "guilty" when my entire hand went to the pocket to ditch an item. This method allows for the dirty hand to appear as if it never goes out of sight, while getting rid of the coin in a very expedient manner.

THE DENIM DITCH

While concentrating all of your attention on your left hand, the hand that is supposedly holding the coin, you say:

> *"I'll keep it right out here in front. It won't go anywhere near the pocket…"*

Hold your left fist out in front of you. Allow your right thumb, along with its palmed coin, to enter your right pants pocket, as if you are simply striking a relaxed pose (fig. 12). This position will only be held for a beat. With the outstretched right fingers, give the outside of your pocket three quick pats. The thumb-palmed coin is released into the pocket, as the fingers make this

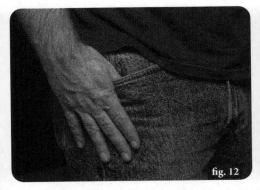
fig. 12

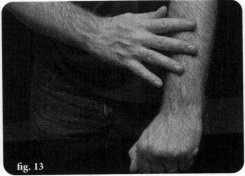
fig. 13

patting action. The empty right hand then immediately comes up, crosses in front of the body, and pats the left forearm, to show that you will not be using sleeves either (fig. 13). I rather like the reverse psychology of ditching to the pocket, while explaining that this is exactly what you are not going to do. The "heat" comes off of the pocket and is redirected toward the left arm or sleeve.

"...or use my sneaky sleeves, or anything like that."

ONE-HAND CLAP

Now, you will utilize a little ruse that really does a lot to reinforce the idea that your hand is holding a coin, when, in fact, it is empty. Shake your left fist as if it were loosely jingling the coin inside. Raise your right hand, palm down, about a foot above the left hand. Revolve the left fist counter-clockwise, so that the closed fingers are now facing your palm-up right hand (fig. 14). Pantomime tossing the coin up into your open right hand. As the right hand closes to "catch" the coin, allow its fingers to close flat as one unit. By rapidly closing your outstretched fingers against the base of your left thumb, you will get an audible "snapping" sound (fig. 15). This sound is the supposed noise made by "catching the coin" against your palm. Really snap the right wrist upward as the "catch" is made, in order to properly sell the illusion. By adding the extra sense of hearing to the vanish, you are maximizing the impact of it. Anytime you can utilize multiple senses in your magic, the magic moments will absolutely play that much stronger.

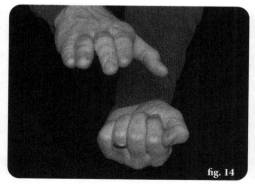
fig. 14

fig. 15

> *"And just like that, the coin melts away like a frozen margarita hidden in your pocket during church service. I lose more money that way!! Damn. I really gotta stop doing that. What a perfectly good waste of a margarita, too."*

Oh Yeah….

As I stated before, these are six individual coin moves that I strung together to form a routine. For whatever reason, I always avoided learning some form of a one-coin routine, so this was as good a reason as any. Each and every one of these moves is versatile and can stand on its own. I would like to say that when I perform The Up and Over Vanish as a stand-alone item, it is usually performed as part of a coin toss. The coin is flipped in the air, caught in the left hand, and slapped on the right closed fist. I say, "Call it in the air, heads or tails." Whatever side the coin lands on, I say something like, "Heads. You win. You get to see a trick," or, "Tails. You lose. Looks like you have to see a magic trick," and then on with the vanish. The entire running time of this routine does not last longer than thirty seconds or so, even though the write-up makes it appear much longer.

```
C:\>
AUTO
REPEAT
DISENGAGE_
```

Effect

A lesson in self-control. The discipline-challenged magician displays a "special" deck of cards with a built-in feature that makes it impossible to ever repeat the same trick twice. To test it, a selected card vanishes from the deck and appears beautifully in the spectator's hand. The effect is attempted again, but due to the "specialness" of this deck, something goes very wrong. Just like that, ALL of the cards suddenly appear in the spectator's hand, except for one measly card—the selection. A technological breakdown of epic proportions, but it's all for your own good.

Needed

A deck of cards and the card box.

Preparation

None

Performance

Bring out the cased deck and show it around as if it were a very valuable item, such as a pricey smartphone or perhaps some sort of diamond-studded monocle case. By the way, I do predict that the monocle will be making a comeback in a huge way, but in the meantime, just hold that deck with tender love and care.

> *"Check it out!! I waited in line all night for this, the brand-new Smart Deck 5.0. I like to stay on top of the latest breakthroughs in close-up card-magic technology."*

Slowly remove the deck from the card case. After placing the deck in your left hand, set the card case down onto the table directly in front of you. It doesn't really matter which side is up or which direction the case is pointing. Its sole purpose is to act as a "mini table", so that you easily pick the deck up off of it with one hand. This can be quite difficult to do straight off of a table, unless you have some type of crazy, superhero-suction fingers. If that's the case, I want to read your magic book.

> *"It comes with a brand-new carrying case. That's pretty sweet. Let's take a look and see how it works."*

Bring your right hand over the deck, preparing to cut off the top half. Act as if the deck is somehow "locked", making it impossible to cut them. Handle the deck as if it were completely glued together.

> *"Give the deck a cut and.... Hmmmmm. Something seems to be wrong with the..."*

Suddenly "remember" that you need to key in the password to make it work and then pantomime doing so. Just give the deck four quick pokes with your right index finger, as if you were keying it in on a smart phone.

> *"Oh, gotta put in the password. And we..."*

Give the deck a few cuts. Feel free to let it rip with any fancy dandy flourish cuts that you have been saving up for a moment like this.

> *"...are...in. We're in!! That is some smooth handling, right there. And let's take a listen to the riffles."*

Use your left thumb to quietly riffle the upper left corner of the deck. The first few times you do this it should almost be silent. Use your right index finger to "turn up the volume" by rapidly pressing the middle of the top card. As you continue to "press the volume button", simply increase the force and volume of your thumb riffles. I find that by bending the right fingertip under the deck so that the fingernail is pressing up against the face of the bottom card, it makes it easier to support the deck while your left thumb does its riffling.

> *"There we go. We've got some riffling, some cutting, and it even has all of the latest features."*

Thumb the top card off of the deck by about two-thirds of its width. Your left thumb will be holding the card in place, side-jogged to the right. Place your right thumb across the right edge of the card as you push the middle of the card upward with your right fingertips, so that when you let go with your left hand, the card will remain locked in a convex bend. By pressing the center of the top card back inward with your right thumb, you will get a great "clicking" sound as it is popped out of its concave position. If this seems difficult, it is not. Just snap the card so that it makes some sort of clicking sound.

"This is shuffle mode. Click it and now we can shuffle as much as we want."

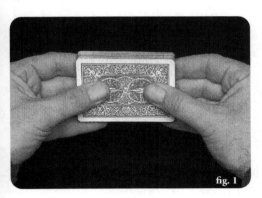

fig. 1

Begin shuffling the deck and then abruptly stop, as if a text message just appeared across the top of the deck. Rotate the deck so that you are now holding it horizontally with both hands, thumbs on top. This is the classic text-message grip (fig. 1). Pantomime typing in a quick text with your thumbs and then realize that you have been "very unprofessional".

"That's fantastic. We are cutting, shuffling, and riffling now. Wait a second, I'm getting something. Ha ha ha!!! That's funny. Let me just respond really quickly. 'LOL.' I'm sorry. That was pretty unprofessional of me. I'm all yours, I promise."

Give the deck one more shuffle and cut before thumbing over the top card for two-thirds of its width, just as before.

"Let me show you my absolute favorite new feature. This is the Auto Repeat switch. If I disengage this switch, I will never be able to repeat a trick, which is the way it is supposed to be. You get in there, do your thing, and then get out. This feature is perfect for me because occasionally, in a moment of weakness, I have repeated a trick and then ended up exposing myself...exposing the trick, not myself, per se."

Repeat entire "popping" card bit, just as you performed it earlier, to "disengage the switch".

"Let's switch Auto Repeat off and see how it works. I'm very excited!!"

Grab the top half of the deck from above with your right hand. Your right thumb riffles off the bottom two cards of the top half and then catches a left pinky break below them (fig. 2). The rest of this top half is lifted off and placed face down on top of the card case. It should hang over the edge of the case enough so that you can easily pick it up with one hand, which you will do in a moment.

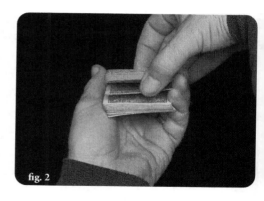

fig. 2

"I'll cut off some of the cards and place them right here on the card case."

Perform a double turnover, showing what appears to be the top card of the deck. Let's assume that the card is the Seven of Hearts (fig. 3). Turn the double face down and thumb over the top card, while continuing to hold the pinky break under the Seven. Insert the supposed "Seven" into the front of the cards in your left hand, out-jogged for about half of its length. Angle-jog this card to the left, just enough so that your left index fingertip can neatly fit between the out-jogged card and the outer left corner of the deck (fig. 4).

"Let's take a look at the card that was cut to, the Seven of Hearts. This will be our trusty selected card. Let's go ahead and put it back into the pack, like this."

Grasp the cards off of the case with your right thumb and fingers, thumb above. Because of the overhanging edge of the cards, this is quite easy to do.

"Now, this is the type of magic trick that is sooooo pretty, it just begs to be repeated. What's so pretty about it, you ask? Oh, nothing really. Just a little bit of this..."

Slap the right-hand cards into a face-up, one-handed fan (fig. 5).

"...Bam!! Actually, that's not really the pretty part. Here, I'll show you."

fig. 3

fig. 5   fig. 6

Instruct the spectator to hold their hands out together, keeping them palm up.

"Hold out your hands together, palm up. This could get freaky."

As you use the fan to gesture toward the out-jogged card, you will be performing The Trashcan Production, which is described in complete detail in "Wannabe Ninja". For explanation's sake, yours and mine, let's go over it as it applies to this routine. First off, do not let the fact that there is a card sticking out of the left-hand cards psych you out. The angle-jog ensures that the card will not get in the way of the mechanics of this move, so don't you worry your magical self.

—————— TRASHCAN PRODUCTION REFRESHER COURSE ——————

As the right hand and its fan move over to the left hand, gesturing toward the "supposed" out-jogged selection, the selected card above the pinky break is going to be levered up at a ninety-degree angle, so that it is now perpendicular with the rest of the deck. To make this happen, you will simply be straightening out your left fingers. The right hand fan obscures the card from view as it is levered up and over. Since the bottom two fingers of the right hand are not involved in the actions of the one-handed fan, they are free to extend to the left to grab the card once it has been turned face up (fig. 6). Once the right fingers have stolen the card, use the fan to trace the path that the card is going to take across your body. Explain that it will go up the arm, across the chest, down the other arm, and into the spectator's hands.

"What I'm talking about is how the card is going to vanish from the pack, travel up the arm, jump across the manly chest, slide down the other arm…"

Tap the spectator's palms with the card fan as you demonstrate where the card will appear.

"…and arrive in your hands. I know, right??"

Hold the fan about three inches above their palms as you push the out-jogged card flush into the deck with your left index finger, sending the card on its magical journey. Trace the path that the card "takes" with your eyes as you are verbalizing the path. If you are proficient at doing The Wave because you were a funky-fresh break-dancer in the 80's, then feel free to rock that out to really show the "card in motion". Just as you tell the spectator that the card is on their palms, snap the fan downward about an inch as you release the card from the right fingers, trapping it in on their palms (fig. 7).

"Here we go. Up, across, down…and into your hands. Oooh, that was nice. I almost HAVE to try it again."

fig. 7   fig. 8

Close the fan in your right hand and place it face down back onto the card case. Take the card from the spectator's palms and tell the spectator that you are going to try to repeat it again as you pretend to put it face down into the back of the pack. What you really do is repeat the TILT Bluff Bottom Placement, as described in "Wannabe Ninja". Very simply, just slide the card to the bottom of the deck, from behind, while "demonstrating" that it is going into the center (fig. 8). Since it is being viewed from the front, the spectator cannot see exactly where the card is really being inserted. Buckle this card or perform a pinky pull-down in order to get a pinky break between it and the deck.

"Let's see if the auto repeat disengagement protects us. Here goes nothing. Again, I shall put the Seven of Hearts back into the middle of the pack."

Pick up the cards on the case with your right hand, as before, and snap them into another glorious one-handed fan. Rotate your left hand clockwise so that the deck is being held with the backs directly facing the spectators, perpendicular to the floor (fig. 9). Gesture toward the cards in the right hand with the fan, but instead of stealing the top card as before, you are going to tilt the left hand downward just enough to let gravity do its thing and to allow ALL of the cards above the break to revolve over face up, where they fall upon the bottom three fingers of the right hand (fig. 10). Since these fingers are not involved in holding the fan, they are free to provide a landing pad for the rolling cards. Again, the cards are not stolen by the right fingers. They fall onto them due to the downward tilting of the left hand. Of course, this "Gravity Roll" should only be performed once the right-hand fan is in position to fully cover the action. Once the rolling cards hit the bottom three

fig. 9

fig. 10

fingers of the right hand, they press the cards upward, trapping them in place against the back of the right index finger (fig. 11). It is important to hold the left-hand card as you would a complete deck. Just be careful to not let the card's exposed right side flash to anyone on your right.

"Gotta admit, I'm feeling a bit nervous. I don't have a warranty or anything on this if something goes horribly wrong. Oh well, let's do it."

Repeat the same tracing of the card's path with your eyes as you did before while describing the card's journey. When you say "onto your hand", gently release the clipped cards with a downward snap from underneath the fan, right onto the spectator's palms (fig. 12).

"Up the arm, across the chest, down the arm, and onto your hand... is the rest of the deck. Huh?"

This "kickback card climax" comes as a big surprise to the spectator. They are expecting one card to show up on their palms, not a whole pile of them. First, they will feel the heavier weight of the cards and then they will recognize that it's the rest of the deck. Close the fan in your right hand and dribble the cards face up onto the cards in their hands, as well.

"Well, if that's the rest of the deck, then yes, you guessed it."

Focus all of your attention toward the left hand as you re-grip the card between the left thumb and index finger. Give the card a sharp flick with the left middle

fig. 11   fig. 12

finger and then turn it face up to show that it is the selected card. When you show that the selection is the only card remaining in the left hand, well, that is a very strong moment. And of course, strong moments make for strong magic.

> *"Well, if that's the rest of the deck, then yes, you guessed it. This must be the Seven of Hearts."*

Take the deck out of the spectator's palms and then add the single card to the top of the deck. Shake your head in disappointment as you put the deck back into its case.

> *"Hmmmmmmm. I guess there's no repeating with this one. I knew I shoulda got that warranty."*

BREAK'N

Oh Yeah....

First off, I need to give a 5.0 shout out to Caleb Wiles for suggesting that the cards appear on the spectator's palms. Originally, they plopped back onto the card case, spilling off the table, landing in someone's beer, etc. It was a mess. Thanks, Caleb, for cleaning up the joint. You've got class.

This is one of those routines where the importance of the script is paramount. Just have fun with it. These gags work, and better yet, they also provide for a wonderful psychological "disarming" of the spectator's guard. The sheer "goofiness" of the opening bits of business absolutely lead the spectator down a very deceptive path. It's obvious to them that these jokes are not the makings of some super serious stuff. There's a certain air of "whimsicalness" that really sets up the smack of the "kickback card climax". David Williamson, Ray Kosby, and many others have also published fantastic routines containing a "kickback card climax", because they are cool like that.

Well Traveled

Cameron Francis

Effect
A four-Queen packet is shown. One is selected and placed into
the pocket. It turns out this selected Queen is very good at
making a fool out of the magician as she repeatedly jumps from
the pocket back to the packet. The spectator lends a helping
hand by holding on to the other three Queens, as the selected
lady is placed into the pocket one last time. Like a jealous ex-
love that just won't go away, she suddenly appears all by herself
in between the spectator's palms. And the other three Queens?
Well, they are each removed from three separate pockets.

Needed
A deck of cards

Preparation
None

Performance
Take out the deck of cards and openly remove the four Queens, tabling them
in an alternating red-black, face-up fan.

> *"Well, since I do love the ladies, here is a little ditty with the four
> Queens: Clubs, Diamonds, Spades, and Hearts."*

Ask the spectator to name their favorite of the four Queens. Let's assume that
the Queen of Hearts is chosen. Cut this chosen card (Queen of Hearts) to the
face of the fan. Pick up the fan and hold it between your right thumb and
fingers, with the faces toward the spectator.

> *"Go ahead and choose one of them if you would. The Queen of Hearts?"*

Tap the face of the Queen of Hearts with your left index finger.

> *"Oh boy. Well, I didn't really want to bring this up but the Queen of
> Hearts and myself, well, we kind of have a history..."*

Lower your right hand down so that the cards are now face down,
parallel with the ground.

You are now going to perform an Elmsley Count under the guise of reversing the cards' order, apparently bringing the chosen Queen from the bottom of the packet up to the top. The Elmsley Count, invented and first published under the name The Ghost Count in Alex Elmsley's *Four Card Trick* manuscript (1959), is an extremely popular and wonderful false count that accomplishes two things. First off, it can be used to count a small packet of anywhere from three to six cards as four. Second, during the count, the third card is never shown, so it could actually be face up and it would not be seen.

To perform, the right hand continues to hold the face-down packet by its right edge, with the thumb on top and the fingers below. The left thumb approaches the top card of the packet and peels it into the left hand for the count of "one" (fig. 1).

The left hand takes its card a little bit forward and to the left of the right-hand cards. As this is happening, the right thumb pushes all of the cards except for the bottom one to the left. These two cards should be pushed over as one single block. The left hand comes back to the right in order to take this two-card block as one on top of the single left-hand card. As this two-card block is pushed over, taken, and then held in place with the thumb of the left hand, the original top card of the packet (the card now on the very bottom) is re-taken by the right fingers underneath the single card now in the right hand for the count of "two" (fig. 2, from below).

For the count of "three", the left hand moves back toward the right-hand packet and uses the thumb to peel the next card onto its cards. As this card is peeled into the left hand, in-jog it in order to hold a pinky break below it (fig. 3).

Lastly, the remaining card in the right hand (the original top card of the packet) is taken by the left thumb on top of the other three for the count of "four".

It is important that you keep your right hand in a fixed position during the count. It should be stationary and not move at all while the left hand is peeling off the cards. Equally important to the effectiveness of this move is keeping a nice, smooth pace or rhythm while counting. Don't be in a hurry. This count should look no different than if you were really reverse counting the cards.

"Yeah, she caught me shuffling with one of the other Queens. Ever since then, it's been completely hellish."

Pull up slightly on the in-jogged card with your right thumb as you push it square with the packet. This will create a small gap for you to get a pinky break underneath the top two cards. Since you "reverse-counted" the packet, the spectator now believes that the top card is their chosen Queen, so "show" them that is the case by performing a double turnover, turning the top two cards face up as one. Thanks to the pinky break, this double turnover is a piece of cake. The chosen Queen (Queen of Hearts) shows, so all is copasetic.

"She's not just the Queen of Hearts. She's also the Queen of Passive-Aggressiveness."

Out-jog this double for about a third of its length (fig. 4).

"She does this thing where pretends that she's not listening to a word I say, when I know she is."

fig. 1

fig. 2

fig. 3

fig. 4

Rotate your left hand palm down and grip the short end of the out-jogged double with your right thumb on top and your fingers below. Allow your left pinky to butt up directly along the short end of the face-up cards.

With the first two fingers of the right hand, push the bottom card of the double, the chosen Queen of Hearts, flush with the two face-up cards. Your

left pinky acts as a "stop", allowing the chosen Queen to line up perfectly with the rest of the cards in the packet as it is pushed in (fig. 5). Immediately pull the indifferent card out from the packet, keeping it face down. This excellent move is known as the Down's Change from *Card Manipulation, Issue Two* by T. Nelson Downs & Newton Hall (1933).

fig. 5

Place this face-down indifferent card into your right, front, pants pocket, being careful not to accidentally show its face in the process.

Keeping the packet face up, re-grip it so you are holding it by its right side, with the right thumb on top and fingers below. You will now show that all three cards are face-up Queens by performing Edward Victor's E-Y-E Count, from his marketed *E-Y-E Routine* (1955), as follows: While maintaining your grip along the right long edge of the packet, use your left thumb to take the top card into left-hand dealer's grip (count "one"). Bring this card underneath the packet as you apparently take the next card on top of it. What really happens is that the left-hand card is left underneath the packet as your right thumb performs a block push-off with the two cards above this deposited card, taking them into the left hand. This block push-off action is the exact same procedure as the second card counted during an Elmsley Count (count "two"). Lastly, take the last card on top of the two cards in the left hand (count "three"). Obviously, don't call out the names of the Queens as you count them. The same Queen is shown twice, but since you are using court cards with a lot of distracting, busy ink on them, the specific identities of each of the cards counted will go unnoticed.

"And I'll keep these three lovely Queens in a nice sexy packet in my hand. Of course, the Queen of Hearts really hates this, as she pretends not to hear me say 'pocket'. She hears 'packet', or at least that's what she says she hears."

Snap your fingers or perform some other dazzling magic action and then Elmsley Count the packet again, apparently showing three face-up Queens with one face-down card among them. Out-jog this face-down card as it is counted.

"And then she just shows up in the packet...uninvited. Awkward."

As you grip this out-jogged card in your right hand in preparation to remove it from the packet, lift up on it just enough to allow your left pinky to catch a break above the bottom card. Take out the out-jogged card and then turn it face up onto the face-up packet, showing that the selected Queen (Queen of Hearts) has jumped back to join the other Queens.

"Yup, there she is. Jealous much?"

You are now holding a pinky break below the top two cards of the packet, creating a double. By lifting up on the face-down Queen as you removed it and catching your break at that time, you eliminated having to perform any type of get ready in order to easily handle the double. Grip the right edge of the double with your right fingers and thumb and out-jog it for about a third of its length.

"Naturally, it's a little upsetting."

Rotate your left hand palm down and once again perform the first part of the Down's Change, the pushing in of the lowermost card. Remember to let your left pinky act as a stopping guide for this card as it is being pushed in flush and even with the top card of the packet.

"I just cannot seem to shake her."

Before removing the out-jogged card, you are going to rotate everything end for end, re-gripping the two-card portion of the packet in between the right fingers and thumb. This will allow you to remove the out-jogged card with your left hand and to place it into your left, front, pants pocket, remembering to keep it face down in the process (fig. 6). An important note to consider is that when placing the card into the pocket, you don't want to specify which pocket you are placing the card into. Just simply say "pocket". Nobody is going to ask you why you didn't put the card into the same pocket as before, but at the same time, don't go out of your way to point it out to them.

> *"Maybe if I tell her to go to the pocket and wait, and I promise to talk with her later, that'll do the trick."*

Hold the two-card packet face down along its right edge in between the right fingers and thumb, fingers below. The selected Queen (Queen of Hearts) is the bottom card.

> *"Now, hopefully, I can concentrate on these three hotties over here."*

You will now count the two cards as three by removing the top card with the left thumb, taking it into left-hand dealer's grip. This is performed on the count of "one". On count "two", the left-hand card is brought underneath the right-hand card, where the right fingertips grip its right edge, as the left thumb pulls off the top card into left-hand dealer's grip. Again, this is the same action as count "two" of an Elmsley Count (fig. 7). The final card in the right hand is pulled with the left thumb onto the card(s) in the left hand, for the count of "three".

> *"But not for long. I saw the Queen of Hearts wink at me from the pocket as she said, 'Meet you at the packet...our packet.'"*

Transfer the cards back to the right hand, gripping them along the right edge between the thumb and fingers, with the thumb on top. Make some sort of snazzy magical action in order to "send the selected Queen back to the packet". This will be accomplished by counting the two cards as four. You will perform this count exactly the same as the previous two-for-three count, but you will exchange cards underneath the packet twice, not just once. These exchanges are performed on counts two and three, not just on count two as in the previous two-for-three count, but for the sake of completeness, here is a better description for you.

The first card is removed with the left thumb and slid into the left hand on

fig. 6 fig. 7

count one. On count two, the left-hand card is carried underneath the card in the right hand and the right fingers then re-grip the cards' right edges as the left thumb pulls the top card into the left hand. For count three, repeat the exact same procedure you performed during count two. Finally, the right-hand card is pulled onto the card(s) in the left hand, for the count of four.

"And just like that, she shows up back in the packet with the other three."

Holding the two cards as four in left-hand dealer's grip, turn the top card face up to show the selected Queen of Hearts has once again returned to the packet.

"What a psycho! I know she's doing this just to absolutely get a rise out of me. And you know what? It's working."

Turn the Queen of Hearts face down and get ready for the easiest Top Change you are ever going to perform.

"I can understand why she's so upset. After all, I'm a close-up magician, a very hot commodity."

You want it to look as if you simply turn the Queen face down onto the packet and then place it into your right, rear, pants pocket. What really happens is that as soon as the selected Queen is turned face down, your left thumb clamps down on top of it, holding it in place in left-hand dealer's grip, as the right fingers pull the bottom card of the two away from the left hand, as if it were the Queen of Hearts (fig. 8). Place this non-selected queen into the right, rear, pants pocket, again being careful not to show the face of the card in the process.

Bring your right hand over the card in your left hand (the Queen of Hearts) and adjust it as if you were simply squaring up the three cards that are supposed to be in there. Gesture toward the spectator with your palm-up right hand, asking them to open up their flattened palm as well (fig. 9). In right-hand Biddle Grip, remove the card(s) from your left hand and place "them" onto the spectator's open palm, and then ask them to cover the card(s) with their other hand. For the nervous-nellies out there, you need not worry at all that the spectator will be able to feel that they are only holding one card between their palms. This simply will not happen.

Pat the right, rear, pants pocket that you just placed the "Queen of Hearts" into with your right hand as you point toward the spectator's hands with the left.

fig. 8   fig. 9

When the spectator goes to check out the Queens that should be in between their palms, they will absolutely freak out for sure when they discover that they are now only holding on to their selected Queen of Hearts.

At that point, slowly remove each of the other Queens from their respective pockets.

"…all the way into the pockets. There's one, there's another, and finally, the other."

Take back the Queen of Hearts, add it to the other cards, place them into your pocket, and take your well-deserved packet-trick bow.

"The Queen of Hearts. What a freak. You know what? Actually, I think I love her."

Oh Yeah….

First off, an incredible thank you to Cameron for allowing me to publish his ultra-fine routine, as well as giving me permission to make a few changes in the overall handling to fit my performance style. I love this routine for many reasons, most especially because all of the pocket loading is completely done wide out in the open. In Cameron's original routine, the selected Queen only jumps back to the packet once before the big switch-a-roo finish. He utilized a cool "underground" two-for-three count and a Gambler's Cop to get the job done. I wanted to add the two extra returns of the selected Queen, as well as eliminating the Gambler's Cop because I can become a whiny baby when it comes to such palming situations. I strongly encourage you to check out Cameron's original handling from his Moment's Notice #7 release for a more detailed explanation of how he gets down with it. Of course, this most-excellent routine/plot is based on Dai Vernon's "Travelers" from *Stars of Magic, Vol. 6, No. 3* (1950).

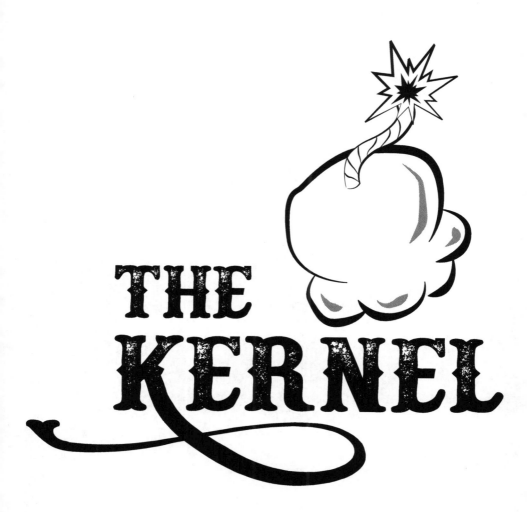

THE KERNEL

Effect
The performer grabs ahold of an unpopped kernel of popcorn. The kernel is placed in the hand, where it is vigorously shaken up and down. Suddenly, a "pop" is heard and the hand is opened to reveal a fluffy, edible piece of popcorn.

Needed
A box, bag, or bucket of popcorn.

Preparation
None

Performance

While enjoying a delicious snack of popcorn at the movies or any other social gathering, reach into the container with your left hand and search out an unpopped kernel, otherwise known as an "Old Maid". When you find one, also grab ahold of a small-to-medium size, fully-popped piece of popcorn and get it into left-hand finger palm as you bring out the "Old Maid" to display (fig. 1, from behind).

"Did you ever wonder why they call these unpopped kernels 'Old Maids'? It's because these are what's left at the bottom of the box, after everyone else has picked over all of the good ones; the undesirables, destined to live a life of solitude. Kind of mean, wouldn't you say?"

Transfer the "Old Maid" to your outstretched right hand, which is held palm up, directly over the container of popcorn (fig. 2).

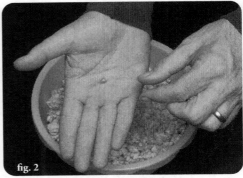

fig. 1   fig. 2

Close your right hand into a loose fist. During the act of turning your right fist palm down, allow the unpopped kernel to fall out of the bottom end of your fist, back into the container (fig. 3). If you adjust the container with your left hand, or simply move it out of the way as the kernel is dropping into it, you will disguise any sound that is made when the "Old Maid" falls in. Tightly squeeze your right fist around the "supposed" kernel.

"All we need to do is apply a little bit of heat. We do that by squeezing. Something tells me that this 'Old Maid' hasn't been squeezed in a very long time."

Loosely cup your left hand and place it over your right fist, keeping the popped piece concealed underneath your left fingers. Your left third finger should be running perpendicular across your right knuckles (fig. 4). Make sure that your left fingers remain together so that you do not flash the popped kernel now on the back of the right fist. Be careful not to apply too much pressure on the back of your right fist or you will break the concealed piece of popcorn.

fig. 3

fig. 4

"Maybe even a little more heat, since it's been oh so very long for this 'Old Maid'."

While keeping your hands in this position, you will now need to vigorously shake both hands up and down, as if you were "air popping" the kernel. Make the movements big and bold, although your hands should never move any higher than the middle of your chest (fig. 5). It is important that during this shaking process, the underside of your right hand is not seen. Keep the backs of both hands facing the spectator, as you shake them up and down.

"We need to get her tossing and turning in there, cranking up the heat. Oh baby, baby. Can you feel it?"

When you feel like the tension has built up and you can't stretch it out any longer, you are going to simulate the popping sound of a kernel of

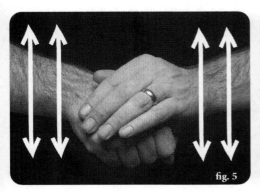 

fig. 5   fig. 6

corn by simply snapping your right fingers, with one loud, crisp "snap". This action is hidden in two ways. The first is that your left hand, if properly oriented toward the audience, acts as a great cover. The second way is by utilizing the philosophy that the larger action covers the smaller action. In this case, the larger action of shaking your hands up and down covers the smaller action of snapping your right fingers (fig. 6, from below).

"A little bit more and a little bit more and..."

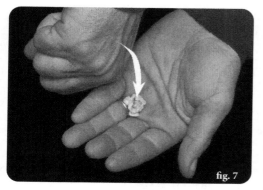

fig. 7

As soon as the popping sound has been made and has registered in the audience's mind, turn your left hand palm up and roll it just to the left of your right fist. At the same time your left hand turns over and opens up, you will roll your right fist to the left. This will cause the piece that is sitting on the back of the right fist to fall into your open left palm (fig. 7). Start to open up your right fist as soon as the piece of popcorn falls off of it, as if you just tossed it from the right fist.

"WOW!!!! Did you hear that?"

As soon as the piece has hit your left palm, toss it right back onto your right palm. Immediately, toss it right back into your left palm again. Keep doing this back and forth, as if you were trying to prevent it from burning your hands. It's kind of like playing a game of Hot Potato with yourself.

"Ouch! She's pretty hot now! Scorching!! Well, what did you expect after all this time alone? Of course, she's good to go."

Pick up the piece in your right hand and let everybody see that your hands are otherwise empty. I usually toss the piece high into the air and catch it in my mouth, a trick I learned to do as a kid (I knew it would pay off someday). You could just as easily choose to simply put it directly into your mouth, but what's the fun in that, I ask you?

"That is one PILT: Popcorn I'd Like To Taste. Never count the old maids out. Never."

Oh Yeah…

I love this routine!!! This is one of those perfect "right time, right place" routines. It reminds me of Superman squeezing a piece of coal until it turns into a diamond. In fact, that could be a very cool presentation angle for those inclined. I have been chasing this effect for over ten years. I originally utilized a gimmick consisting of a piece of bubble wrap glued to one side of a Zippo lighter. The bubble wrap method proved to be too much set up work, plus I longed for an impromptu method. After that, I believe I tried some crazy method involving popping one of my knuckles, but since I did not want arthritis to set in just yet, I searched for a bigger and better way. Snapping your fingers is the perfect sound. It cuts through nicely and is invisible, since there are no hidden gimmicks. Give it a try. It's not as "corny" as you may think. It's also not very hard to pull off at all. In fact, it's a snap!!!

And if anybody steals my original bubble-wrapped Zippo gimmick, then we are going fifty/fifty on that bad boy!

One
little
letter _____a_____

YOU MUST BE
THIS TALL
TO RIDE

Effect

A weird transposition. The word "Here" is written on the back of a card and it placed "over here". The word "There" is written on another card, and it is placed "over there". The letter "T" is crossed off of the word "there" and added to the word "here". It appears as if now only the words have switched places, but as the cards are turned over, they have physically switched places as well.

fig. 1

Needed

A deck of cards and a marker.

Preparation

Write the word "THERE" across the back of a playing card (fig. 1). Place this card second from the top of the face-down deck.

Performance

Give the deck a few casual shuffles that will keep the top two cards where they are. I usually do a Riffle Shuffle while wearing a pair jeans and a nice tee-shirt, because I'm all about casual. Of course, you could certainly get the job done with a Hindu or an overhand jog shuffle if you like.

> *"Have you ever heard of the term 'orthographic neighbor'? Almost sounds a little dirty, doesn't it?"*

Slowly spread the cards from hand to hand, being careful to not expose the writing on the back of the second card.

> *"Actually, orthography is the study of the spelling systems for specific languages. Things like 'I before E, except after C', spelling rules, long and short vowels, silent consonants, and all of that other wonderful stuff."*

Separate your hands so that each hand is holding its own small spread of cards. Alternate gesturing with each spread, as you say each of the following paired-word examples.

> *"An orthographic neighbor refers to a set of words that differs from each other by only one letter—Slob/Snob, Bull/Ball, Card/Cord..."*

Square up the cards and then hold them in your right hand as you bring out the marker from wherever it lives.

> *"...Pen/Pan."*

Perform whatever false cut it is that floats your boat. For me, I float easy with a simple double undercut False Cut. Briefly, holding the deck from above in right-hand Biddle Grip, swing the top half of the deck into your left hand with your right index finger (fig. 2). Replace the right-hand cards back onto the cards in the left hand, catching a pinky break between the halves. By the way, if this feels like you have just performed a Swing Cut, you are right. Again, re-grip the deck from above in right-hand Biddle Grip, transferring the break to your right thumb. Your left hand takes half of the cards below the break and cuts them up to the top of the deck. This action is repeated with the remaining cards below the break. There's your false cut, you sneaky little you.

> *"Doesn't sound like much, but sometimes one little letter can make all the difference in the world. Throwing a ball up in the air is not the same as, say, throwing a bull up into the air. One of those is going to leave a mark."*

Perform a double turnover, displaying the top card of the pack; for example, the King of Diamonds. This should not be treated as a selected card. You are just cutting the deck and turning over the "top" card. Since you will be turning this card(s) over a couple of times, it would be in your best interest to keep the double out-jogged, or better yet, catch it in the Altman Trap by allowing the fleshy pad of your left thumb to rest between the double and the rest of the pack after the card(s) has been turned over (fig. 3, from behind). By pushing the ball of your left thumb to the right, the double will side-jog to the right as well. This makes it very easy to take that double into your right

fig. 2   fig. 3

fingers and to do whatever it is that you think you need to do with it, but I recommend turning it face down again and placing it back onto the deck in the Altman Trap, because that's how this trick works.

> *"Here's another example for you. On the back of this card, the King of Diamonds..."*

Pick up the marker and write the word "HERE" on the back of the top card (fig. 4), the supposed King, and again, perform a double turnover and have the King signed across its face. After the card has been signed, perform a KM Move with this double. There really is no difference in handling from the original two-card version of the KM Move. However, because I dig you, let's run it here. Briefly, the thumb and first two fingers of the right hand grip the face-up double by its right side, with the thumb on the face. Drag the card(s) to the right until the left fingertips contact the back of the double. The left hand then turns palm down and moves away to the left with the face-up deck and the back card of this double, while the right hand now only holds the

fig. 4   fig. 5

face-up King (fig. 5). Ladies and gentlemen, the KM Move.

> *"I'm writing the word 'HERE' and we will place it...here. What a coincidence!!"*

Place the King face up onto the table to your right, so that the "T" written on the back is closest to you. Status check: this King has the word "THERE" written across the back of it, but you are in a wonderful position because the spectator believes that it says "HERE", when in fact the "HERE" card is now on the bottom of the face-up deck.

Transfer the face-up deck to your right hand, where your right thumb can lift up the back of the top card and catch a break beneath it. The rest of the right fingers hold the deck in Biddle Grip. You need to perform another double undercut, transferring the card on the face of the deck to the back of it, as previously described. This places an indifferent card on top of the "HERE" card.

> *"Let's grab another card..."*

Turn the deck over so that you are now holding it face down in right-hand dealer's grip and perform another double turnover to show that this top card, for example, is the Two of Clubs.

> *"...the Two of Clubs, and write down its location as well."*

Turn the double face down, remembering to catch it in Altman Trap, and write "THERE" on the back of the supposed Two, which is really an indifferent card. Make the letters look the same as the "THERE" card that you previously wrote out. Perform one last double turnover and have it signed across its face as well.

When this has been completed, catch a left pinky break below the double. Repeat the exact same KM Move as before and then table the Two to your left. The deck now has a "THERE" card on the back (top) card of the deck.

"I'm writing 'THERE' because I'm placing the card there."

If you perform one last double undercut, transferring the face card to the back, you are automatically set to repeat this trick again. You are welcome for that, but for now, place the deck away, as it is not needed for the rest of the routine.

"Now, in this example, the difference between here and there is one little letter 't', but that really can be a huge difference."

Pick up the King on the right and place it face up into right-hand dealer's grip. Your right fingers should be obscuring the "T" and most of the "H", which is good because you are going to be miscalling this card as the "HERE" card. Tilt the face of the card toward yourself, so that the writing is facing the spectator (fig. 6). They see the "ERE", and since you are passing it off as the "HERE" card, everything is super cool and as it should be.

"Imagine if the object of your desire said to you in a sultry voice..."

You are going to do a funky version of the Mexican Turnover, often referred to as the Wild Card Move, which I picked up in *The Secrets of Brother John Hamman* by Richard Kaufman (1989). This two-handed approach is far less scary than the one-handed approach, which is the norm for Three Card Monte games that occur on the streets of New York City. (They need one hand free so they can rob you blind with the other.)

fig. 6   fig. 7

We will get the job done as follows: the right hand slides its face-up King beneath the face-up Two on the table. Your left fingers keep the left side of the face-up Two momentarily locked in place, as your right thumb contacts its face as well (fig. 7). Both cards are then lifted up by the right hand and turned palm down. As the right hand turns over, its fingers push the "THERE" card, the King, into the open left palm. Use the corner of the card in the right hand to point at the writing on the card in the left hand (fig. 8). Make sure that the spectator only sees the backs of the cards during the switch.

"'...or do you want to go over THERE...with me?' You'd want to get that one straight."

Status check again: your ever-loving spectator believes that the "HERE" card on the right is the King and that the "THERE" card on the left is the Two, when in reality, they are the other way around. Man, we are sneaky!

fig. 8

"But then again, sometimes you'd rather be 'there' than 'here' or vice versa."

To make the cards "switch" places, scribble out the "T" on the left. Don't

fig. 9

fig. 10

be subtle about this (fig. 9).

> *"So, if we wanted those two cards to switch places, we could simply cross out the 'T' on the 'THERE' card, the Two, so that it now says 'HERE'".*

Next, add a big, bold "T" to the card on the right (fig.10). Explain that the Two is now "HERE", pointing to the scribbled card on the left, and the King is now "THERE", pointing to the card on the right.

> *"Then we could add a brand new 'T' to the 'HERE' card, the King, making it 'THERE'. Pretty amazing, huh?"*

Of course, your spectator will be suspicious and think that all you have really done is simply switched the letters around, not the cards. They might even try to punch you in the face, or at the very least, call you on your oh-so-very-lame brand of magic.

> *"I know that it looks like all we did was change the writing on the backs of the cards, and that's not really going to cut it. But check it out..."*

Slowly turn over each card, one at a time, and reveal that you are the "goods" because you DID make them darn cards switch places after all.

> *"...the Two that was once 'THERE' is now here and the King who was once 'HERE' is now undeniably there—a genuine orthographic miracle!!!!"*

Give the spectator the transposed cards as the greatest souvenir of their lives. Put the pen back from where it originally came.

> *"Man, that kind of wiped me out. I think I need a catnap, which of course, is not the same as a cab nap. Falling asleep in a taxicab will get you arrested every single time. Trust me, I know from personal experience."*

And remember as I stated before, because of the last Double Cut that you performed earlier in the routine, you are wonderfully reset to rock this routine again. Of course, if you have no interest in the reset, feel free to omit that final Double Cut. I won't call you bad names.

Oh Yeah…

I really wanted to come up with a two-card transposition, but one that had a definite visual moment to signify that the cards had changed places…as well as being done with a sense of humor. The concept of moving a letter from one place to another was probably first inspired by the most amazing alphabetic superhero out there, Letterman, from The Letter People. That, my friends, is one obscure reference for you. He was faster than a rolling "O", stronger than a silent "E", able to leap a capital "T" in a single bound. He removed that letter "T" from his varsity letterman's sweater in order to make the magic happen, and now so can you. So can you!

Effect

Two of the greatest presidents in the history of the United States of America are put through a popularity contest as a penny and a quarter go through a series of amazing transpositions. Six back-and-forth phases of patriotic goodness go down before they suddenly fuse together into one twenty-six cent piece of something weird.

Needed

Two matching quarters, two matching pennies, and a very strong adhesive. If you are "super", use Super Glue; if you are "crazy", use Krazy Glue; and if your name happens to be "Elmer", use Krazy Glue.

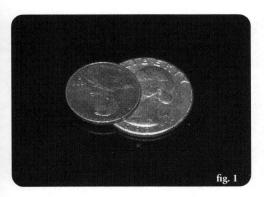
fig. 1

Preparation

Place the quarter on a flat surface, head-side up. Place a "blob" of the glue on the middle of the left side of the quarter, right next to George's nose. If you need the exact measurements of a "blob", technically, it's somewhere between a "smidge" and a "splat". Pick up a penny and place its far right side onto the glue, head-side up as well (fig. 1). For purposes of explanation, we shall refer to this glued set of coins as the "QP" gimmick. Place the QP in your left pants pocket, the remaining quarter and penny into the right pocket, and you are set.

Performance

"When I ask, 'Who are the greatest presidents of all time?' I get lots of answers. But for me, it's a 'no-brainer'. Without a doubt, it's gotta be James Buchanan and Franklin Pierce. I'm totally serious. Just kidding. It's George Washington and Abraham Lincoln. I'm a fan. I even have these rare metal engravings of their likenesses. Got them on eBay for about twenty bucks each…which is a total steal. Here, I'll show you."

Reach into your right pocket and bring out the two coins. Hand them to the spectator to examine. Odds are they will not be terribly impressed.

"Open up your hand and check 'em out. I kind of have a bond with these two great men."

Point to the quarter with your left index finger.

"Sometimes I'm feelin' a bit George and other times..."

Continue pointing to the quarter as you pick up the penny and display it at your right fingertips.

"...straight up Lincoln. It's kind of hard to pick a favorite."

———————————— PHASE ONE ————————————

This first transposition phase is called "The Flying Shuttle Transpo". The basis of this transposition revolves around a move independently created by Larry Jennings, Danny Korem, and Jay Sankey, entitled "The Flying Shuttle Pass". This version of a shuttle pass allows for some movement of the coin as it lands while apparently being tossed from hand to hand, giving a great illusion of realism.

To perform, take the penny and execute your best false transfer into the left hand. I always perform my Arcade Vanish, which is fully described in "Coins à la Carte" in this very book. Of course, any type of French Drop or Retention Pass would also do the trick. Whatever route you choose, the penny should end up in right-hand fingertip rest. If you utilized the Arcade Vanish, simply release the coin from right thumb palm to fingertip rest. After the false transfer, the left hand is held in a loose fist, with the back of the hand facing upward. Gesture toward the left hand, saying:

"Abe was our sixteenth President."

Pick up the quarter from the spectator's palm between your right thumb and index finger. The penny is secretly hanging out in fingertip rest, so keep it covered by the right fingers. Continue to hold the quarter in this position as you display it a few inches above the spectator's palm.

> *"George was our first. So, I guess that makes him my right-hand man."*

Curl the right index finger in toward the palm, carrying the coin into thumb palm as the hand settles into a loose fist.

> *"But then again, George also sells himself out on that teeny little one dollar bill, while Abe is sitting pretty on the five, so maybe Lincoln should be the right one."*

Make a "magic" twitch between the two hands to signify that something freaky just went down. Your right hand drops the penny into the spectator's open palm, while continuing to hold the quarter in thumb palm. The second that the penny hits their palm, shake your left fist, preparing to show that it now "has" the quarter. Release the quarter from thumb palm into fingertip rest as you bring your right hand a couple of inches toward the left hand, which should be winding up to gently "toss the coin". The back of your right hand should be facing the spectator as the left fist turns slightly to the left, and then rolls back to the right as you pantomime gently tossing the quarter into the right hand (fig. 2). As the "supposed" coin makes its imaginary flight to the right, turn your right hand palm up, dropping down an inch or so in the process. Thanks to the wonderful world of inertia, as the hand turns over, the coin stays in contact with the right fingertips for a fraction of a second before falling back down into the waiting right palm (fig. 3).

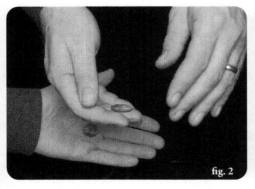 

fig. 2   fig. 3

Yes, this transposition phase is a total bluff, as the spectator never actually sees the quarter inside of the left hand. The shaking of the left fist just prior to the toss implies that it now has the quarter. A fraction of a second later, the spectator sees the coin falling from the left hand into the right, so all is good in the neighborhood.

"See what I mean?"

PHASE TWO

The second transposition phase is called "The Fisticuffs Transpo". One coin is placed into the fist, the other on top of it. Under a covered shake from the other hand, the two coins instantly switch places. This transposition has always reminded me of a close-up Substitution Trunk illusion. The overall look of this phase has some similarities to other penny/quarter transpositions already in print, most notably "Loose Change" by Scott Robinson. His awesome effect was originally published in both of his sets of lecture notes *Varied Methods and Last Night At The Round Table*. A big presidential "thank you" to Scott for allowing me to throw down my version.

Perform some effective retention pass with the quarter into the left hand, while secretly retaining it in the right. Again, I elect to perform my Arcade Vanish, leaving the quarter in right-hand thumb palm. After the false transfer, the left hand holds its supposed coin in a loose fist, with the back of the hand facing uppermost.

"George was a tall man, about 6'1"."

fig. 4

Transfer the quarter from thumb palm back into right-hand fingertip rest position as you reach forward to pick up the penny from the spectator's palm. As you pick up the penny between your thumb and index finger, use your remaining right fingers to press the quarter into classic palm. Place the penny onto the center of the back of your left fist (fig. 4).

"But Abe looked down at George from above, at 6'4"...without the hat. So, I guess that puts him on top."

Point to the underside of your left fist with your right index finger, as you say:

"But then again, George was a brave general in the army, as well as a noble farmer, the backbone of America."

Now, point to the penny on top of your fist, saying:

"Abe...was a lawyer, and then a politician. I think we know what to do with this one. Switch!"

To make the coins switch places, contact the penny with the ball of your right thumb as the right hand covers the back of the left hand from view. You will now be performing Bruce Berkowitz' variation of the L'Homme Masqué Load utilized in his routine "Odd Coin Transit" (*Coin Magic* by Richard Kaufman, 1981), which itself is actually based upon an earlier move of Ross Betram's. To do this, slide the penny with the ball of your right thumb toward and into the open thumbhole of your left hand. This is made even easier by slightly rolling the left hand forward so that the thumb hole is diagonally pointed toward your face as the penny is slid toward it (fig. 5). Once the penny has fallen into the thumbhole, roll the left hand back downward slightly, so that the thumbhole is now facing your body. This will make the back of your left hand a nice flat surface on which to release the classic-palmed quarter (fig. 6). You can help camouflage the smaller secret mechanics of this transposition by giving both hands one big up and down shake as you perform the dirty work.

fig. 5

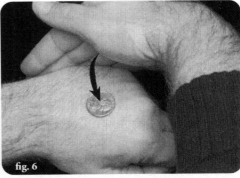
fig. 6

Remove your right hand to show that the quarter is now chilling most magically on top of the fist. Pick up the quarter in your right fingers as you turn your left fist palm up, opening it to show that it now contains the penny.

—————————————— **PHASE THREE** ——————————————

This third transposition phase utilizes your pocket instead of your closed fist, and because of that, we shall refer to it as "The Pocket Rockin' Transpo". By the way, I totally love coming up with names for effects, in case you hadn't noticed by now. Our secret friend, the "QP" gimmick, gets to join in on the fun. So, without any further ado, let's go rock some pockets.

It's time to put all those hours of coin roll practice to good use. With the quarter, perform your very best one across the knuckles of your right hand. Allow the quarter to complete its roll right into the spectator's palm. If you simply cannot do a coin roll, then you could just flip the coin into their hand, but what's the fun in that?

> *"George was a very handsome man and a fabulous dancer. See?"*

With your right fingers, pick up the penny from off of your left palm and show the heads side to the spectator, as you say:

> *"Abe was what they refer to as 'facially challenged'..."*

Re-grip the penny with the left fingers and place it on the back of your right thumbnail, in preparation for a coin toss. Flip the coin into the air, and then catch it in your left hand. This may feel weird because normal protocol for catching a coin during a coin toss is to do so with the opposite hand than the one that initially did the flippin'. But remember, we are not normal. We are magicians. Enough said.

> *"...and no one could ever make heads or tails of his dance moves."*

Now, once the coin has been caught, turn the left hand palm down and slap the coin onto the back of the right hand (fig. 7). This will set you up to perform the Up and Over Vanish, found in "Coins à la Carte" from the very book you are reading right now. Since it is described in detail there, I will give it the briefest of descriptions here. Ready? After the coin has been tossed, caught, and slapped, the ball of your left thumb drags the coin into the thumbhole of your right hand, where the penny can then fall into fingertip rest position. This happens as the left hand "supposedly" slides the penny off of the back of the right fist. And there you have it.

Place this "penny", really just the empty left hand, into your left pocket. As a subtle convincer, I always give the outside of the pocket a tap with my open left hand after I have removed it.

> ### "So...we'll just put him into the deep dark corner of my pocket."

While keeping the penny concealed in finger palm, pick up the quarter with your right thumb and index finger and display it at eye level.

> ### "But even George knows this..."

You will apparently toss the quarter from the right hand into the left, but in reality, you will repeat the actions from the first phase of "The Flying Shuttle Transpo" by curling the right index finger in toward the crotch of the thumb, carrying the quarter into thumb palm. Of course, this curling of the finger is covered by the right hand's larger action of winding up to toss the coin. As soon as the thumb has clipped the quarter, release the penny from finger palm, letting it fly it into the waiting left hand (fig. 8), which then immediately closes into a fist around it. This is essentially "The Bobo Switch" from *Modern Coin Magic* by J. B. Bobo (1952).

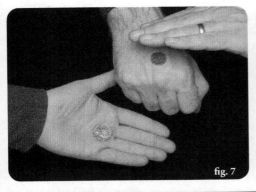 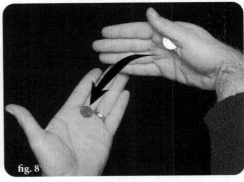

fig. 7   fig. 8

Tap your left fist against your left pocket to signify that "magic" is happening. Allow the quarter in the right hand to drop out of thumb palm, landing in finger palm as you slowly open up your left fist to show that it now contains the penny.

"...nobody puts Abey (rhymes with baby) in the corner."

Hold your right hand up at chest height, horizontally, and with its back toward the audience. With your left fingers, place the penny between the right thumb and the top edge of the first finger, around the first joint (fig. 9). Reach back into

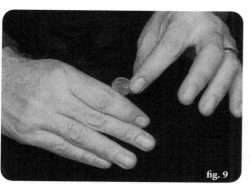

fig. 9

your pocket with your left hand and remove the QP gimmick, and hold it in the same position as the penny in the right hand, with the quarter end upmost and outermost (fig. 10). The penny end of the gimmick is being hidden by the left index finger (fig. 11, from behind). Note how both hands are mirroring each other.

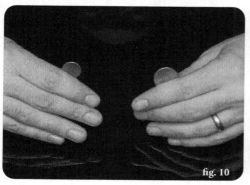

fig. 10

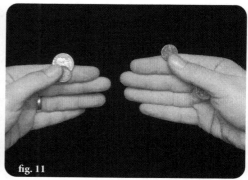

fig. 11

─────────────── **PHASE FOUR** ───────────────

This next phase is a lightning fast visual transposition of the two coins. Thanks to the QP gimmick, you will see that you can change the right-hand coin with a just a flick of the finger, but we will get to that in a moment. For now, let's dive headfirst into "The QP Tipover Transpo".

Extend your right hand forward, bringing the penny and the finger-palmed quarter just above the spectator's open palm. You are now prepared to rock yet another quasi-"Bobo-Switch" into the spectator's hand. But first, focus your attention on the penny, saying:

> *"Maybe we can settle this by looking at their character? Abe was known as 'Honest Abe' and that's pretty rare for a politician, so I guess that puts him ahead. But then again..."*

Shift your attention back to the exposed quarter-end of the QP gimmick.

> *"...we all know that George cannot tell a lie. Just ask that cherry tree."*

It's time for the switch, "Bobo" style. Curl that right index finger inward again, carrying the penny back into thumb palm as you release the coin from finger palm into the spectator's hand. I like to obscure their view of their own hand by keeping my right hand held out flat, directly above the coin that was just dropped (fig. 12). As you remove your right hand, give their hand a little tap. The spectator will always look down at their hand afterward. Use this misdirection to swing your left middle finger from in front of the penny end of the gimmick to directly behind it (fig. 13, from behind). By releasing pressure with the left thumb and pushing forward with your left middle finger, the QP gimmick will tip back toward you as it's clipped between the index and middle fingers (fig.14, from behind). Transfer the tip of your left thumb to the edge of the gimmick closest to you and press it in toward the middle finger. This will cause the penny end of the QP to snap off of the underside of the right index finger so that the gimmick ends

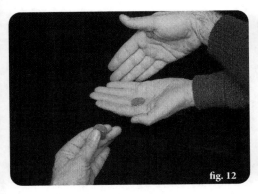
fig. 12

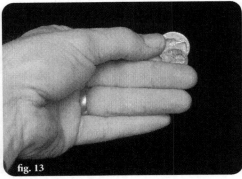
fig. 13

up flat against the right index and middle fingers, quarter side out. Push the QP up with your left thumb, showing as much of the penny end of the gimmick as possible, without exposing any of the quarter which is now hidden behind the fingers. When the spectator looks up after being misdirected by the coin change in their hand, they will be absolutely amazed

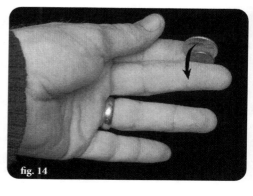

fig. 14

when they see the penny in your left hand staring right back at them.

"Man, it's really hard to choose."

PHASE FIVE

This concludes the straight-up transposition phases of this routine. I hope you enjoyed yourself. I would now like to welcome you to the wonderful world of "Lil' Georgie Come Back". It is during this and the sixth final phase that you will be unloading the single coins back into your pocket, while at the same time setting up for the big fusion finish.

Pick the quarter up from off of the spectator's hand with your right thumb and index finger. This is easy enough to do while continuing to keep the penny in thumb palm. Display the quarter for a beat before placing it into your right pocket. Again, I usually give the outside of the pocket a little tap to imply that it is in there, which this time, it actually is. Once again, the thumb-palmed coin should not impede this action at all.

"George came from a very well-to-do family with lots of wealth saved and passed down through generations. Very deep pockets."

While holding your left hand out in front of you, focus all of your attention toward the exposed penny-end of the QP, as you say:

"Abe, on the other hand, was definitely not high society. Born in Kentucky, he was dirt poor, and raised in a log cabin."

Allow the QP to fall from your fingertips into the palm of your left hand. Close your left fist around the gimmick as it lands on the palm, being careful to not let the spectator see the gimmick.

"I think they have a name for that now, something like 'Trailer Trash'. We probably could just throw it away."

Look down at your right pocket (the one that supposedly contains the quarter), saying:

"But then again, Washington did have those gnarly wooden teeth, which is pretty trashy as well."

Wave your right hand, which still has the penny in thumb palm, over the left fist in major magical way. Open up the fist to show that the quarter has just shot back from your pocket to join the penny.

"So, maybe he's not worth hanging on to after all."

PHASE SIX

It's time for the penny to show that it, too, can make the epic leap from pocket to fist. Like a proud papa, I give to you "Abe's Final Return".

With your left thumb, slide the QP to the tips of the left fingers so that the quarter end of the gimmick is protruding from them. This happens as you turn the left hand so that the back of it is now facing the spectator (fig. 15). Bring your right hand, with its back also showing to the spectator, behind the fingers of the left hand. Use the screen of your left fingers to hide your right index and middle fingers as they clip the penny from the crotch of the thumb. As the right fingers straighten out, they drag the penny out from behind the quarter-end of the gimmick (fig. 16). This will look exactly as if you simply took the penny from out of your left hand and into your right.

"I don't know. Maybe we are nitpicking now."

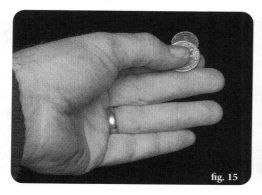

fig. 15

fig. 16

Display both "coins" at the fingertips, as you look toward the "quarter" in the left hand (fig. 17).

"Let's see. George is first on Mt. Rushmore. Absolutely the place to be."

Switch your gaze back to the penny in the right hand as you allow the QP to drop back into the closed left fist.

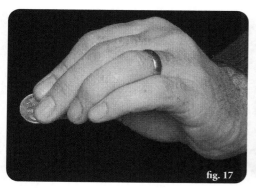

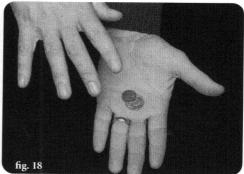

fig. 17

fig. 18

"Abe is dead last, almost like a pathetic afterthought."

Place the penny into your right pocket as you shake your left hand containing the "quarter".

"So, it's gotta be George. Definitely George!!"

After removing your empty right hand from the pocket, bring it over to the left hand fist and make a mystical wave.

"But then again..."

Open up your left fist to display the penny side by side with the quarter (fig. 18).

"Abe did have that totally sweet beard. So, who really knows anymore?"

Point to each of the two coins with your right index finger. Cupping the left hand slightly allows the gimmick to lie more naturally in the hand, as it puts a little bit of the palm's flesh directly underneath the top coin of the gimmick (fig. 19). Without it, the coin might appear to be balancing at a crazy angle, which is an entirely different effect altogether.

"If only there were some way to honor these two amazing presidents. Perhaps some sort of wacky holiday where the banks would close and all of your favorite stores would have huge sales, proudly commemorating these presidents' special day. Oh yeah, I guess that's called Presidents' Day."

Wave your right hand over the gimmick. This is your final magical moment, so do it proud.

"I was thinking something more like an amazing 26-cent salute that fuses together the best parts of each of these two great men into one patriotic shiny clump of presidential metal, like this."

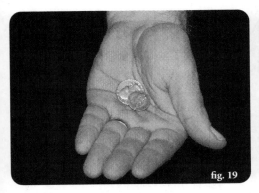

fig. 19   fig. 20

Snap your right fingers over the gimmick and then give your left hand a sudden jerk upward, causing the QP to hop off of the left palm and onto the right one. Repeat this gentle tossing action back into your left hand and then, slowly and ultra-fairly, pick up the QP with your right thumb and index finger by the edge of the penny end of the gimmick to display the fused weirdness that has suddenly set in (fig. 20).

> *"I pledge allegiance to the coins of the United States of America. God bless the USA!! Too much?"*

And for all of the table workers out there, you will notice that when you put the QP back into your left pocket, you are automatically reset to do it again and again and again.

Oh Yeah...

This routine is a MONSTER!! There is a lot of magic happening in a short amount of time. The write-up to this routine reads much longer than the actual running time of the performance. I am very fond of the overall construction of this routine, but of course, use the individual phases on their own, if you must. I highly recommend performing the entire routine, script and all. For those that love a good cheat sheet, here is a list of the order of the phases:

Flying Shuttle Transpo, Fisticuffs Transpo, Pocket Rockin' Transpo, QP Tipover Transpo, Lil' Georgie Come Back, Abe's Final Return, and of course, the granddaddy final meld finale.

And one last thing. My apologies to the families of Franklin Pierce and James Buchanan, as well as the entire state of Kentucky. Them are just jokes there!!!

White Light
White Heat
White Card

Shaun Dunn

Effect

A brilliant display of thought transference, performed in three illuminating phases.

White Light

A prediction of a soon-to-be selected card is placed onto the table. A participant thinks of a number between one and twenty and secretly counts off that many cards from the top of the deck. Even though the packet of cards is completely hidden away from view, the exact thought-of number is somehow revealed like a spotlight in the dark!

White Heat

The secret number is then used to count down from the top of the deck, arriving at a random playing card. The heat is on as the tabled prediction and the selected card are compared to one another. They are exact matches!

White Card

With thoughts flying all over the place like this, some are bound to cancel each other out. In this case, it's each and every card that cancels out, as the entire deck suddenly turns completely blank!

Needed

A blank-faced deck of cards, a regular deck of cards with the same back design as the blank deck, a small piece of paper, and a pencil.

Preparation

Remove a card to be predicted from the regular deck. In this case, the prediction will be the Jack of Spades. Draw a light pencil dot on both the upper left and lower right corners of the back of the card (fig. 1). The best way to do this is to make sure that your pencil is very sharp, and as you lower its tip onto the corners of the card, give it a series of back and forth twists between your fingers. This will make a nice, defined, "secret-agent" pencil dot. Trust me. I am a professional something-or-other.

Place this pencil-marked card into the blank deck at the twenty-first position from the top. Put the blank deck into an easily accessible pocket. If you wear a coat or a hoodie, the front pockets are perfect for this. I do not keep the cards in the case while in the pocket. Just place the uncased deck neatly into the pocket so that you can ring it into play when the time comes.

Take the small piece of paper and write your prediction on it, which of course is the same as card number twenty-one in the blank deck (Jack of Spades)…but you knew that already (fig. 2). Fold up this prediction into quarters, keeping the writing on the inside, and place it somewhere convenient. Take out the regular deck and let's get it on like Donkey Kong.

fig. 1

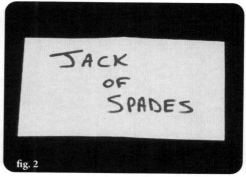
fig. 2

Performance

You are going to begin with a funny, little bit. I mean, really, what better way to start, right? Look your participant square in the eye and very seriously ask the following question:

> *"Have you ever been so connected with somebody that every time you go to finish a sentence, they finish it for you?"*

As soon as your participant starts giving their answer, jump in and interrupt them loudly and abruptly "finishing their sentence" for them.

> *"Yes!"*

Nail the timing on this interruption and it will really get a great response. Afterward, act shocked and amazed by this "coincidence".

"Wow! Would you look at that?"

Take out the folded prediction to display before setting it onto the table, or some other place in full view.

"I think there's a connection going on here. That should make this much easier. I had a thought earlier, so I wrote it down, folded it up, and then prayed to the stars above that I'd actually have a reason to use it."

Bring out the regular deck of cards and hold it in left-hand dealing position.

"Actually, this is one of those ESP, Extra Sensory Perception, mind-reading thingies, or whatever the kids are calling it these days. Now, we all have thoughts—good ones, bad ones...dirty ones."

Depending on the "good-time, party attitude" of your participant, deliver the next line as if you are subtly hinting toward their wild side. If they happen to be a nun or something, just imply that it is targeted at yourself.

"Some dirtier than others."

Casually begin to spread through the deck, displaying the faces of the cards as you speak.

"But that's alright. We've got a lot of different thoughts all mixed up together, flying around in our minds, much like the condition of this deck of cards—all mixed up."

Close the spread and hand the deck to your helper, inviting them to shuffle the cards nice and well.

> *"But some of us are more mixed-up than others. I'm not sure whom I'm referring to here, you or me? But do me a favor and mix those cards up any way that you like. When you are done, let's take a look at what kind of 'mix' we are dealing with here."*

Take back the cards and spread them face up so that your participant can see the fine results of their shuffle efforts (fig. 3).

> *"Fantastic. Very thorough and, most importantly, very well mixed. A mixed-up deck for all of our mixed-up thoughts."*

Square the face-up deck back into your dealing hand, as you point to "the thoughts up in the sky" with the other.

> *"But our thoughts aren't just floating around in our minds. They go up into the atmosphere, mixing together with everyone else's mixed-up thoughts."*

Gesture toward your helper to let them know they are now going to actively participate in this experiment.

> *"So attempting to read minds can obviously be pretty tough to do, so it's a good thing I won't be doing it alone."*

Re-spread the pack between the hands one last time.

> *"When it comes to reading minds, it obviously takes two people. Reading your own mind isn't nearly as impressive as it may sound."*

Up-jog both a red card and a black card as you spread through the deck.

> *"It takes a sender and a receiver to get the point across."*

Take ahold of the spread solely with your left hand, as your right hand points to each of the two up-jogged cards.

> *"Some people are natural senders. Some are natural-born receivers."*

Tap the "sender" card (the first card that you pointed to just a second ago) as you talk about senders, before pushing it back into the spread (fig. 4).

"A sender puts out a very strong thought. Think of them as really loud talkers, but instead of using their mouths, they use their minds. Perhaps you know someone like this?"

Point to the up-jogged "receiver" card as you continue your rant about receivers. When done, push it back into the spread.

"I, myself, am a natural-born receiver. I can pick up pretty much anything up there. As a kid, I even picked up free cable TV, which of course, made me very popular in the neighborhood."

Square up the spread and turn over the card so that you are holding the face-down deck in left-hand dealer's grip.

"You are usually one or the other, but rarely both. That being said, I'm going to try to demonstrate what might happen if somebody did possess both of those incredibly amazing skills."

Instruct your helper to think of any number between one and twenty.

"Please think of a number between one and twenty. That's twenty different choices you have, right? Make it a good one."

fig. 3

fig. 4

While they are focusing in on their selected number, you are going to switch out the regular deck for the blank one using the most stealth-like secret switch I know. You ready? Here goes. Turn around so that your back is facing your helper, put the real deck in your pocket, and then take out the blank deck in its place. Of course, these blatantly bold actions are completely covered as you are simply explaining to your participant what exactly it is you want them to do. Part of that explanation involves the participant turning around "so the magician doesn't see how many cards are being cut off". You are simply providing a visual aid as part of your instructions. Nothing more, nothing less. There are a million deck switches out there. Use what you like, but I love doing the dirty work wide out in the open, with my back facing the audience. That makes me smile from the inside out.

> *"Now, listen. I would like you take this deck and then to go ahead and turn your back on me. Don't worry. You won't be the first person to do that to me, or the last."*

While you are doing your "back-turn deck switch", you will give your participant a few more instructions to follow regarding how they are going to be utilizing their specific number to count off cards from the top of the deck. You are about to jump headfirst into the Ten-Twenty Force, first published in Billy O'Connor's "After The Four Ace Trick" in *The Magic Wand*, Vol. 24 (1935). This is a wonderful method for forcing a card, based upon a glorious mathematical principle.

To perform, tell the spectator to take their thought-of number of cards off of the top of the deck and then to place this small packet face down onto their right palm. For example, if they thought of the number thirteen, they would turn their back and spread thirteen cards off of the top of the deck onto their right palm.

> *"While your back is turned, take your thought-of number and spread off exactly that many face-down cards from the top of the pack onto your other palm. Try and do it as silently and with as little motion as possible. Don't even move your lips. This is where all of those years of silent ventriloquism are going to pay off."*

Turn back around so that you are now facing your helper again and go over the process one last time before turning them loose with the deck.

> *"So if you were thinking of the number thirteen, silently push off thirteen cards into your other hand. Got it?"*

At this point, the participant takes the deck, turns their back toward you, and then silently counts off the selected number of cards from the top of the pack onto their other open palm. Again, let's assume the thought-of number is thirteen.

> *"OK. So you are now holding a confirmation packet of cards in one hand that equals the same number as the secret one in your mind."*

Ask your helper to then hand you the rest of the deck while their back is still turned. Once done, they are to place their now-empty hand on top of their "secret-number packet", creating a "secret-number sandwich" between their palms, and then finally to turn around and face you.

> *"Now, before turning back around, reach behind you and hand me the remainder of the deck. And once you've done that, go ahead and cover up your 'secret packet' between your palms and then go ahead and face me again."*

While holding the deck in left-hand dealer's position, explain to your participant that you are now going to attempt to listen in to the inner voice in their mind. Explain that since they thought of a number between one and twenty, you are going to count off twenty cards onto the table. Ask them to think the word "yes" when you deal the card that corresponds with their selected number.

fig. 5

> *"I am going to deal twenty cards onto the table, just like the twenty choices you had when you thought of your 'secret number'. When I deal the card that lands on the number you are thinking of, I want you to say 'yes' to yourself. Try not to make a noise, blink, or do anything at all that might tip me off. Just say 'yes' to yourself, inside your mind. Ready?"*

As you count aloud from one to twenty, deal the cards onto the table in a messy pile, one on top of the other (fig. 5).

"One. Two. Three..."

As you deal the cards onto the table, keep an eye out for the pencil-marked force card. Once you see the pencil dots, remember the number that it landed on. In our case, since the thought-of number is thirteen, you will see the pencil-marked card get dealt at position "eight". Remember that number as you finish dealing the rest of the cards. Because of the nature of the Ten-Twenty Force, you will be able to reveal the thought-of number by simply subtracting the number that landed on the pencil-dotted card (in our case, eight) from the number twenty-one. This gives you a total of thirteen, which is their thought-of number. Here's another example for the math majors out there. If the marked card was dealt on the number three, you would subtract three from twenty-one to get the thought-of number eighteen. Got it? Great!

"...Eighteen. Nineteen. Twenty."

Explain the fairness of what just went down and then look your participant in the eyes as you dramatically reveal their number. Again, in our case, it's the number thirteen.

> *"In your head, you said 'yes' to one and only one number. Because I am such a natural receiver, I picked up on it very easily. You are thinking of the number thirteen."*

Have your helper lift off their hand off of the packet of cards and count them face-down onto the table, once again confirming this awesome display of mind reading.

"Not bad, huh? Well, like I said before, receiving is really a piece of cake. It's the sending of messages that has always been a little tricky for me. But let's go for it while I'm still all tuned in and stuff."

Place their thirteen cards on top of the face-down deck. Next, square up the pile of twenty cards on the table and add them to the top of the face-down deck as well, as you explain how you plan on going about proving your ability to send a thought of your own for successful pickup.

"Now, I am very familiar with this particular deck of cards, maybe even a little too familiar some might say. I had a very specific feeling that you would think of the number thirteen. In fact, I knew exactly which card would ultimately end up in the thirteenth position from the top of the deck, even after you did all of that shuffling."

Point to the prediction that has been lying on the table for the entirety of the routine.

"I would like to point out once again that I placed this prediction here before we even touched the deck. I point this out because basically I'm insecure and really want your admiration."

Hand the deck to your helper and have them count to their thought-of number (thirteen) by dealing the cards one at a time from the top of the deck, just as you previously did.

"Do me a favor and take this deck of cards and count down to your

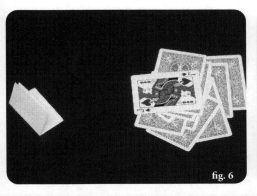

fig. 6

fig. 7

number thirteen. Just go ahead and deal them into a face-down pile."

Because of the mathematical nature of the Ten-Twenty Force and since the cards were previously dealt down in reverse order, meaning card one is tabled, card two is placed on card one, etc., that thirteenth card (or whatever their thought-of number is) will be the pencil-marked card that matches your prediction. What an amazing thing of Ten-Twenty beauty.

Once the thirteenth card has been dealt, instruct your helper to turn it face up.

"OK, now please turn over that thirteenth card and see what landed at your thought-of number."

After your helper turns over the card that landed at their random, thought-of number (Jack of Spades), state the card's identity (fig. 6).

"The card at the thirteenth position is the Jack of Spades. Hmmm. Very interesting. I set out to send a thought-of card to you and I wrote it down on this piece of paper."

Invite them to pick up the piece of paper and to open it up to show a perfect matching prediction written upon it (fig. 7).

"Please open up the prediction and read what thought I wrote down before sending it successfully to you. Yes!!! The Jack of Spades."

Hand both the prediction and the Jack of Spades to your helper as you pretend to wipe off your brow.

"Man, that one just about wiped me out. Sending is much tougher than I expected. But in actuality, there is a reason that one cannot easily send and receive psychic messages. You see, every thought message cancels out every received message, and if you do it too much..."

fig. 8

With as much magical gusto as you can muster up, slowly turn the deck face up to reveal that every single card has amazingly turned completely and utterly blank (fig. 8).

"...you end up cancelling everything out...and I do mean everything!"

Oh Yeah...

This routine is obviously very influenced by one of the most incredible card routines out there, the modern day classic "Overkill" by Paul Harris, a totally killer piece of close-up entertainment that was originally published in Close Up Fantasies Book One (1980). "Overkill", which features individual ideas by Allan Ackerman, Theo Bamberg, and Ed Marlo, needs absolutely no improvements. That being said, Shaun's pencil-dot addition to the effect allows for a true stunning moment of psychic entertainment to occur. The blank deck and all of its commercial appeal doesn't hurt things either. If you are opposed to a blank deck for reasons that I can't figure out, you could draw a giant "X" on every card except for the force card, saying "you knew it wouldn't be these cards since they are cancelled out." Shaun also shared the wonderful fact that this effect could be performed with a borrowed deck. Basically, you would note the 21st card from the bottom (face) of the pack. Write down that card as your prediction. Everything else is the same except that you perform the entire routine with the cards face up.

Feel the light. Feel the heat. Feel the card. Yes, feel the card.

The 80's Called... They Want Their Magic Book Back

Effect

A signed and selected card is revealed to the spectator by explaining the inner workings of an old code system in which words or shapes are folded together to reveal a secret message. After the code is "cracked" and revealed, the indifferent card magically turns into the actual signed selection.

Needed

A deck of cards with a Nine of Diamonds, which is going to be destroyed each and every time that you perform this routine, so... start stockpiling those Nines, or better yet, maybe you could simply start stealing them out of your magic buddies' decks. If you have really tough magic friends, perhaps consider omitting that previous step. Lastly, get a black magic marker and you are set.

Preparation

Remove the Nine of Diamonds, the Eight of Spades, and the Four of Hearts from the deck. Place the Nine face down on top of the pack. Place the Eight and the Four face up in the third and fifth positions from the top, respectively. So, the order from the top: Nine, indifferent card, face-up Eight, indifferent card, face-up Four, rest of the pack. After completing this massive setup, wipe the tears from your eyes, pick yourself up from off of the floor, and let's do this thing!!

Performance

Give the deck a few good riffle shuffles, while at the same time being careful not to expose the two face-up cards near the top, saying:

"I used to be a member of a Young Magician's Club back in high school. Five members, including myself. Let's just say that there wasn't much of a waiting list to join. Geeks with cards, but WE thought we were cool. It was run by one of the history teachers, Mr. Tricks. He didn't really like magic at all. I think he had gotten stuck with our group solely because of the name. Besides, Mr. Wonder had just retired the year before."

After completing the shuffles, place the deck into left-hand dealing grip and loudly start to riffle up the back of the deck with your right thumb, getting louder with each riffle. Do this enough times so that there is no question that you are now just being annoying. Deliver the following line as if you were trying to compete in volume with the deafening sounds coming from the deck.

> *"I know we were obnoxious kids and all and we could get kind of loud, but one day, out of the blue, Mr. Tricks lost it and yelled..."*

Abruptly stop riffling the cards, as if a needle were just scratched across a record album. If you are not a DJ or are under the age of 25, go look up the term "record album". Go ahead. We'll wait.

> *"That's it!! No more Young Magician's Club. No more finding selected cards, producing rabbits, or any of that other funny business. It's over!"*

Pause for an extended beat, to allow the silence to sink in, and then say:

> *"So, I'm like, 'Whoa! What is this, Footloose High? You can't do that. This is America.'"*

Defiantly give the deck one slow, but loud riffle...to "prove your point".

> *"We have the right to find selected cards, play with rabbits, or do anything else that will completely obliterate any chances that we might actually have of being popular in school...if THAT is what we want to do".*

Allow your left thumb to lie across the top card of the deck, the Nine, as the right hand lifts off about two-thirds of the pack. The left thumb slides the Nine to the left, onto the remainder of the deck, while holding a pinky break directly below it (fig. 1). Your right hand completes the "cut" by dropping its cards back onto the rest of the deck in the left hand, retaining the break below the Nine.

Congratulations! You have just performed a Slip Cut, and don't you feel like a better person for it?

"So, Mr. Tricks made us a deal. He said, 'OK, I'll tell you what. If you can find my selected card without actually "finding" the card, the club can continue. But if you fail, it is over.' Sounded like a trick...from Mr. Tricks. OK, how do you find a card without actually 'FINDING' the card?"

Now, you will need to force the Nine of Diamonds on a spectator, but do so with love. I use a variation of Gary Oulette's Touch Force (*Close Up Illusions* by Gary Oulette, 1990). Briefly, the cards above the break are spread face down from hand to hand, being careful not to reveal the reversed cards near the top of the pack. This is best accomplished by doing a block push-off of the top six or eight cards. Just use your left thumb to push that small block of cards as one unit by their left edges into the right fingers, as you begin spreading the cards above the break. The spectator touches the back of one of these cards. It is out-jogged for half of its length, and then close the spread back into the left hand. The right hand then approaches the deck from above and pushes the out-jogged card flush with the deck, as it lifts off all of the cards at the break (fig. 2). The Nine is on the bottom of the right-hand half. Of course, a standard riffle force will get the job done, too.

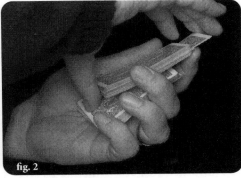

fig. 1   fig. 2

"He touched the back of a card and signed his name across the face of it. For explanation's sake, will you please do the same for me?"

While continuing to hold the bottom half of the deck in your left hand, remove the Nine with your left fingers and hand it to the spectator. Tell them to make sure that they do not show the face of the card to you, as you hand them the marker to sign their name across it.

Have the Nine replaced back onto the cards in the left hand and hold a pinky break above it as you replace the right-hand cards back on top of everything. Cut the cards at the break (or Double Cut if you want twice the magical-cutting power), controlling the Nine to the top of the deck and putting the face-up cards into the middle.

Snap your fingers, wiggle your ears, break into some light-hearted demonic chants, or just riffle the cards to show that something "strange" has happened. Spread the top ten cards or so, and then with your left thumb, push cards one at a time into the right hand until you come to the face-up Eight of Spades. Thumb it onto the table and perform another block pushover, concealing the face-up Four of Hearts as you finish spreading the rest of the cards into your left hand (fig. 3).

After squaring the cards, give them yet another one of your famous magic riffles and then spread the cards again to reveal the face-up Four in the middle of the pack. Thumb it off directly to the right of the tabled Eight (fig. 4). As you close the spread into your left hand, obtain a pinky break below the top two cards of the deck.

You are going to want to show the top card of the deck, the Nine, to be an indifferent card. In order to achieve this Herculean task, perform your best double turnover, which is now slightly less Herculean than it could have been, thanks to the pinky break that you were so very smart to hold (fig. 5). Point out to the spectator that this "top" card (the Ace of Clubs in our case) is just a random card that will be used to help find their "selected" card.

> *"When using the Selectigami Code, these two face-up cards contain the message, or 'The Payload'. The next club member's job was to take a random card from the top of the deck and to write down the 'payload' cards on the back of it, like this."*

————— **THE WRITING SEQUENCE** —————

Turn the double face down and draw an "8" and a Spade symbol on the top third of the card. Draw the "8" as two circles stacked on top of one another, and not in the typical infinity-like "figure eight" style (fig. 6). The Spade symbol is essentially an upside-down heart with a cute, little stem sticking out from between its "heart

fig. 3

fig. 4

fig. 5

fig. 6

bumps". Make the drawings extra dark and thick by tracing over them a few times.

"The Eight of Spades..."

Next, draw a "4" and a heart symbol on the bottom third of the "indifferent" card (fig. 7). Notice how the bottom of both the "4" and the heart are proportionally a bit longer than their upper-halves. Hand the marker to the spectator and ask them to please put the cap back onto it as you blow on the ink in order to dry it. Use this small window of misdirection to once again obtain a left pinky break below the top two cards.

> *"...and the Four of Hearts. Still no selected card found yet. Do me a favor and throw the cap back on the marker for me. Thank you kindly. Now, this third card is called 'The Carrier'. Pretty interesting, huh? Mr. Tricks didn't seem to be too impressed either."*

Grab the two cards above the break between your right thumb and middle finger. The thumb holds the card at the bottom right corner and the middle finger is on the upper left corner (fig. 8). As you bring the cards up toward your mouth to blow on the ink again, bow the card very slightly. This ensures that the double stays in alignment. Don't make a huge "oversell" of this. A gentle little blow while showing the spectator that this is still the "indifferent" card goes a long way.

> *"Finally, our crack code breaker stepped up to demonstrate the very heart of the Selectigami Code. It is a form of steganography, which refers to hiding a secret code in plain sight, often contained within the folds of the text of something else, like 'The Carrier'. Here we go."*

fig. 7   fig. 8

Drop the double back onto the deck and then use your left thumb to push the single "inked" Nine into your right fingers. Rub the ink with your right fingertips to ensure that it is dry.

"Finding a selected card without finding a selected card."

THE FOLD SEQUENCE

Hold the card in the upper third of its left side, between the thumb and first two fingers of your left hand. Keep the face of the card toward you, being very careful not to flash the card's identity to the spectator. With your right thumb and index finger, pinch the top third of the card in toward yourself, folding it so that the crease runs directly between the two circles of the figure "8". Momentarily hold the fold in place with your left thumb as your right fingers and thumb sharply crease it closed (fig. 9).

Using the first two fingers of each hand, clip the folded third against the rest of

fig. 9

fig. 10

fig. 11

fig. 12

the card (fig. 10). Slide your thumbs inside the fold and push the bottom half of the card up and under your middle fingers, creating a new fold (fig. 11). Roll your hands back toward you so that your palms are facing the floor. This ensures that the spectator only sees the back of the card as you crease that fold into place with both thumbs. You will want to line up the top circle of the Eight with the straight line of the Four until they resemble a Nine (fig. 12). Of course, the top of the Spade and the bottom of the Heart form a very respectable diamond. Smear the fingertips of both hands across the writing, showing that the Nine of Diamonds has just been revealed.

"Your card and Mr. Tricks', the Nine of Diamonds. He had no choice but to let us continue with the club. Before leaving, he asked me, 'What was your part in this little code?' I said that I was the brains behind the operation. He said, 'I doubt that.' Well, that did it. I HAD to save face and show Mr. Tricks just who's boss."

fig. 13

Pause for a beat or two and then snap your fingers. Re-grip the card and slowly turn it face up. Pinch the opposite ends of the card in each hand and pull them away from one another, opening up the card to reveal the actual chosen selection (fig. 13). Man... you are good!

"I went ahead and found his signed card, just because I had to. I lost the club, no more cards, or rabbits. So what? I did gain some self-respect, and THAT's some real magic. Besides Mr. Tricks, silly rabbits are for kids."

Oh Yeah…

A basic idea of this folded revelation was originally inspired by a folding tee-shirt trick of Tom Burgoon's, but for me, its real influence comes from the back page of *Mad* Magazine by Al Jaffe. Growing up, it was always one of my favorite sections of the magazine. It wasn't until many years later that I realized that this awesomely funny tidbit from my youth was actually a very sophisticated form of steganography. A definite seed had been planted. There have been other previously published routines in magic that deal with revealing a selected card or message within the folds of a piece of paper. One of the first was "Cardee Foolee" by Walter Gibson, in The Phoenix, No.9, 1942. Sid Lorraine, Max Maven, Ton Onosaka, and Tomo Maeda have all had published works in this area as well. Big thanks to Joshua Jay for recommending the final change to the selected card. Without that, this trick fell into the "how cute" category, instead of the little magical miracle that it currently is!!!

OUTSIDE
THE
INSIDE

Effect

The word "outside" is written on the outside of a cellophane-wrapped pack of cards. The word is rubbed with a napkin. Instead of erasing, it magically changes to the word "inside", which is now written on the inside of the cellophane, directly on the back of the actual card box itself.

Needed

A pack of cards wrapped in its cellophane wrapper, a dry-erase marker, and a normal permanent marker.

Preparation

Carefully remove the "peel-off" portion of cellophane from the top of the pack of cards, being careful not to tear the main cellophane sleeve in the process. Set this sleeve off to the side. Using the normal marker, write the word "Inside" on the non-flap side of the card box (fig. 1). It is very important that it is written exactly the same as seen in the picture. This regular marker will not be used again.

Pay special attention when writing the "I". It should not be a completely straight line. It should bow to the left slightly.

Also, when writing the "n", be sure to write it as a line that is bowing to the right, butted right up to a "u" shape that is tilted to the left a bit. They are connected at the top of the

fig. 1

fig. 2

fig. 3

right bowed line and the top left of the "u" shape (fig. 2). The reason for the curved lines on the "I" and the "n" is because they will be doubling as an "O" and a "u" later.

Slide the cellophane sleeve back onto the card case. Place a face-down card directly underneath the cellophane wrapper, so that it covers the writing that is on the case (fig. 3). It should now look like a normal deck of cards wrapped in cellophane.

Place the dry-erase marker any place convenient and you are ready to go.

Performance

Show the card case on both sides. Make sure that the audience can see that there is no writing on the case, but don't verbally point that out. The card that is concealed under the cellophane will go unnoticed. If you need a little security, you can hold the case so that your fingertips are covering the edge of the cellophane and the half-moon cutout on the card box.

"And now, for your entertainment pleasure, something guaranteed to bring a smile to your face. Fun with logic. Sounds like a kick, huh? I figured this out while I was studying that in college, before I got kicked out for...that's really not important right now.

Have you ever heard somebody say that you cannot be in two places at one time? Well, I am going to prove that you can, logically."

Take hold of the lower half of the wrapped pack, flap side up, between your left thumb and fingers. Remove the deck of cards from the box, along with the extra camouflage card hidden underneath, with your right hand (fig. 4). Be careful not to flash the writing on the underside of the box.

> *"Notice how the cards are inside the box. Or another way to look at it is to say that the box is outside of the cards, right?"*

Carefully remove the cellophane tube from the card box, but only slide it halfway off of the card case (fig. 5).

> *"And notice how the cellophane is outside the box, or we can say that the box is inside of the cellophane. Got it?"*

Slide the cellophane back onto the box. Place the cards back into the box, continuing to keep the writing on the underside hidden from view.

> *"So, as you can see, the card box actually occupies two places at one time. It is BOTH on the outside of the cards AND on the inside of the cellophane. Logically, we have proved our point...and don't you feel like you are a better person because of it?"*

You are now going to "clear things up" further by writing the word "Outside" on the outside of the cellophane, or at least that is what you want the audience to believe is happening. What you are going to do, in fact, is to modify the word "Inside" that is written under the cellophane by adding dry-erase ink on top of it.

Take out the dry-erase marker and pick up the card case, keeping the word "Inside" toward you, out of the spectator's view.

fig. 4

fig. 5

You are going to turn the "I" and the "n" into an "O" and a "u" by simply drawing two small, curved lines that connect the top and bottom of the "I" to the top and bottom of the left-hand side of the "n" (fig. 6).

The next thing you will do is add a "T" in between the newly constructed "u" and the "s" (fig. 7).

It should now look like the word "Outside". Depending on the brightness of the overhead light, you may wish to actually trace the rest of the letters with the dry-erase marker as well, so that the "shininess" of the ink is the same on all of the letters. This is not necessary, but it does help sell the illusion in some viewing circumstances. Pretend to dry the ink by blowing on it and then turn the card case around to reveal the word "Outside", supposedly written on the outside of the box.

Hold the right end of the case in between the thumb and first two fingers of the right hand, so that the writing is facing you. You are now going to change the word "Outside" to "Inside", simply by wiping off the ink that is on top of the cellophane with your left thumb. This happens

fig. 6

fig. 7

as the left hand approaches the right hand in order to take the case and to lay it down onto the table. To do so, contact the "e" at the end of the word with your left thumb and then simply slide it across the ink to the left, wiping it off completely (fig. 8). Immediately after the wipe, the left end of the case is gripped between the left thumb and first two fingers, where they then table the case with the writing side down.

"But in this troubled world, not everything is always logically accurate. Sometimes when you least expect it, something comes along..."

Snap your fingers and turn over the tabled case to reveal that the writing has now changed to "Inside".

"...and changes the 'Outside' into the 'Inside'. The 'Inside' is now on the outside of the case. How disturbing."

Pinch the non-wrapped end of the case in between the right thumb and fingers and display the writing to the spectator.

"I know it can be very troubling living in a world where outsides can become insides..."

With your left hand, slowly slide the cellophane sleeve off of the card case to show that the ink is now on the inside of the cellophane...outside of the card box (fig. 9).

fig. 8

fig. 9

Again, be careful not to rip the cellophane in the process of removing it. You are clean, clean, clean...and that's a great way to be.

Oh Yeah…

I know that this is kind of a cerebral routine. It is best saved for "sharper" audiences. But no matter how brainy it might seem, there is still enough visual magic to appeal to everyone. You would be best off keeping a brisk pace, not a hurried pace, when performing this routine. The reason is that the longer the dry-erase ink sits on the cellophane, the harder it is to get off.

Now, you are probably wondering how to best disguise a dry-erase marker as a normal marker. The answer? Don't sweat it. It will go unnoticed. But if you are worried about it, there are a number of things you can do. You can wrap tape around the words "dry erase" on the marker or color over them with a permanent marker. Or you can use a Magic Eraser to scrub off the ink as well (See "Magic Eraser" in this book for more on this). Or if you are extremely ambitious and only use Sharpie markers, you can actually crack open a dry-erase marker and remove the ink cartridge. Once done with that, carefully open up a Sharpie and perform an "ink cartridge transplant". Glue it up and you are ready to go. This is something that my main magic man, Joe Cole, did for me and I simply love it. A little bit of hard work goes a long way.

Spoonmelt

Effect

A plastic spoon is melted with the aid of a lighter. This burnt spoon is wrapped up in a napkin and given to the spectator to hold. The spoon is then magically massaged through the napkin, and when it is opened, the spoon has reformed back to its original unmelted condition.

Needed

A cigarette lighter, a napkin, and a cheap, flexible, plastic spoon. You can jump on Amazon.com and search for "light-weight plastic spoons" and I guarantee you will find a plethora of acceptable ones that will work for this effect. I was able to purchase 1000 spoons for the extremely low price of $18.00 from a company called Select Medical that served my "spoon-melting" needs perfectly. That is definitely a lifetime supply. You can also go to any restaurant supply store and feel around until you find a spoon that will work for you.

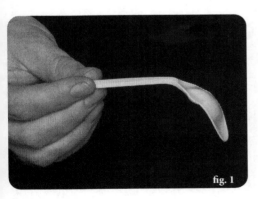

fig. 1

The only prerequisite for the spoon is that you must be able to press on the underside of the bowl and easily push it inside out, so that it "locks" into a position that looks very much like a melted spoon (fig. 1).

Preparation

Place the spoon into your left pocket and the napkin and lighter into your right pocket, or if you are performing in a restaurant-type setting, use the napkin from the table.

Performance

Reach into your left pocket and pull out the spoon. Let everybody get a good look at it.

> *"When I say Uri Gellar, what usually comes to mind? Bending spoons, right? Back in the day, you couldn't call yourself a mentalist unless you could bend one of these babies...with your mind."*

Reach into your right-hand pocket and pull out the lighter, while continuing to hold the spoon in your left hand.

> *"I, of course, have never called myself a mentalist. I'm a magician. So, when I want to melt a plastic spoon, naturally, I use magic. If that doesn't work...I use this lighter."*

Ignite the lighter and slowly move the flame in small circles, about 2-3 inches from the actual underside of the spoon. It is important that the spoon gets hot, but doesn't actually get scorched, so be careful not to let that happen. Hold this position for a few beats.

> *"Now, I don't want to actually burn the spoon. I just want to soften it up a bit."*

Shut off the lighter and then show that the spoon hasn't quite begun to melt yet. Allow your left arm, with its spoon, to drop to the side of your body. Once it has dropped out of frame, your right hand draws all of the attention by igniting the lighter directly in front of your face, making small circles with it.

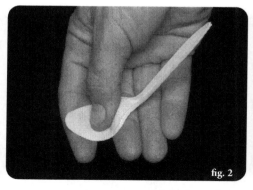

fig. 2   fig. 3

While you are misdirecting by "flicking your Bic", you will press on the underside of the bowl of the spoon, essentially popping it inside out. This is easily accomplished by resting the open side of the bowl directly on your left fingertips and then pressing down with a bit of force in the center of the back of the bowl (fig. 2). It now uncannily resembles a melted plastic spoon.

"The key is to keep the flame moving. That way the heat gets dispersed evenly throughout the spoon. Yes, I have way too much time on my hands."

Bring the "melted spoon" back up to about two to three inches above the flame, but this time, keep the bowl of the spoon pointed directly at yourself (fig. 3). Because the bowl of the spoon is pointing away from the spectator and the back of your left fist obscures the spectator's view of the spoon, the "melted" bowl will go unnoticed.

"Careful not to inhale the fumes or you are gonna be seeing better magic than even I can perform. A little bit more heat and..."

Slowly turn your left fist and its spoon to the right, bringing it into view in all of its "melted glory". If you dip the bowl downward a bit as it is revolving into view, you can further simulate the act of it being melted by the flame (fig. 4). Remember that the flame should continue to be moved in small circles, as you hold the spoon above it.

"...that...should...just...about do it. A bent spoon!!!"

Bring the "melted spoon" up to eye level and show it around at all angles. Dump the lighter into your right pocket as you retrieve the napkin that is in there. If you already have a napkin on the table, use it instead. It is important that the spectator sees that you only have a napkin and a spoon after coming out of your pocket. If you are not clear about this, the spectator may backtrack later and assume that some sort of clever spoon switch took place.

Blow on the spoon as if you were trying to cool it down a bit. Allow the spectator to feel that the spoon is still a little hot, if they so desire, by touching it to the back of their closed fist.

> *"I know that doesn't seem too magical and I did call myself a magician, so maybe I should do something quasi-amazing to earn that title. I think that the spoon may have cooled down by now, but you can still feel a little heat. Here, make a fist. Can you feel that?"*

After allowing the spectator to feel the heat of the spoon, turn it around and place the handle of it into their fist. Very gently and loosely, wrap the napkin around the "melted bowl" (fig. 5).

> *"We'll protect you from any harm by wrapping the hot end in this napkin."*

As you are demonstrating that you want the spectator to rub the spoon through the napkin, "pop" the spoon back into its original shape by pinching the bowl between your first two fingers and your thumb. Press downward with your thumb until you feel it snap into place.

> *"Rub the spoon through the napkin like this. Not too hard. It's still a little hot. Good. Now, imagine that you are somehow massaging it back into its pre-melted state. If you concentrate, you might actually be able to feel the plastic start to harden and mold itself right back into its original, pristine condition."*

Carefully and dramatically open up the napkin, revealing a completely

fig. 4

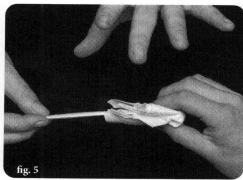

fig. 5

restored spoon. Show it around, but not for too long. You do not want the spectator to press on the underside of the spoon, thus figuring out the secret.

"Take a look. Uri Gellar ain't got nothing on us!!"

Drop the spoon into your left pocket and you are reset and ready to go again.

SPOONIING WITH THE CARPENTER

Card technician, sleight-of-hand expert, and all-around awesome guy Jack Carpenter suggested the following alternate handling. This method of "healing" the melted spoon does not use a napkin for cover. The entire "unpopping" of the bowl happens inside your closed fist while performing something very similar to Vernon's Through the Fist Flourish.

Hold the melted bowl on the palm of your left hand, with the spoon's handle pointed toward yourself. The "popped-up" portion of the bowl should be in a position so that if the left thumb were to press down, you could easily pop it back into place, which you will do in just a second (fig. 6).

Make a loose fist around the bowl as you rotate your left hand so that the fingers are now pointing toward the ground and the spoon's handle is pointed away from you. Reach over and grab ahold of the handle between your right thumb and fingers, fingers on top (fig. 7). Pull the

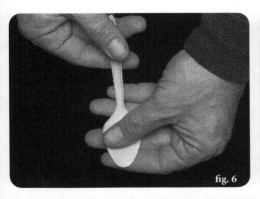

fig. 6

fig. 7

spoon out of your fist and then up and over toward yourself so that the "melted" bowl is being dragged across the back of the left fist. Once the bowl has been dragged past the left thumb, rotate your left hand back so that it is now palm up, bringing you back to your original starting position. Repeat this Through the Fist Flourish once again, returning back to the starting position for a second time. Close your left fist around the bowl for a third and final time. As the left hand revolves palm down, simply use the left thumb to pop the bowl back to its original, unharmed state. As the spoon is pulled around the fist one last time, everybody sees the healed bowl, and suddenly, the world is a better place because of it. Open the left hand out flat and rest the spoon's bowl on the left palm for your final "spoon-melting" display.

Oh Yeah...

I know what you are thinking. Who's gonna be fooled by poppin' a spoon inside out? The answer? Everybody. It is all about context. If you handed a spectator a "popped-out" spoon, without introducing the idea of melting it, they just might stumble on to the solution. The audience is intelligent and aware of the fact that plastic melts with excessive heat. In fact, on a number of occasions, an audience member has beaten me to the punch when the topic of bending a plastic spoon comes up. They have said "Use a lighter" more than once, before the lighter has even been introduced. Basically, they are selling the idea to themselves, all by themselves.

A huge Hot Spoon thank you goes out to my amazing daughter Zoe, who while goofing around after a dish of ice cream, "popped" her spoon and said, "Look, my spoon's melted," inspiring me to develop this impromptu piece. Also, big thanks to Joe Cole for helping with the clean up of this routine, as well as road testing it when I was not as brave as he. Get poppin'!!!

"How in the world did you come up with that?"

"From where do you get your ideas?"

"Do you come up with the method or the effect first?"

If you have ever dabbled with coming up with your own creative and original magic, then you have probably been asked these questions, and a million others just like them. Well, we all have our own weird and wild ways when it comes to summoning inspiration, some that could even get you locked up by the authorities, if you aren't careful. But enough about my problems, right?

The following piece of excellence is described in Francis' own words. If you ever wanted to jump right in and see a detailed example of how the creative process works, keep on reading. This is one heck of an essay and I am super excited to be able to share it with you. And that, my friends, is completely real! So ladies and gentlemen, without any further adieu, here's Francis. -JF

It's sometimes hard to determine the direction in which to go with an idea that has so many fun and plausible possibilities. For that matter, even determining the idea's true source is a challenging but often worthwhile task, as it can shed light on where the idea wants you to take it. Then, when said idea finally makes clear its intentions for you (you're the creative vessel for the greater concept, nothing more), it flits away with a "good luck!" and sits silently, sulkily, obstinately waiting for you to do all of the work to figure out how to make it possible. Ideas can be brats!!

There is surely no one right way of raising an idea (as the analogy to raising a child will by now be obvious), but it always requires a balance of love and firm, experience-driven structure. It also requires patience and a willingness to sometimes shelve the child (now this is just getting weird) until it's ready to work with you, or until you have developed and improved the necessary skills to do the idea justice. Too often, we (or at least I) will attempt something ambitious a little too soon before we're ready. Exercising a bit of willpower to put in the training efforts, practice, and rehearsal before pushing the idea out into the spotlight makes the difference between the audience acknowledging a cute idea and them being blown away by a work of brilliance. The time it takes to bring a piece from conception to standing ovation varies so greatly depending upon the performer, experience, originality, difficulty, funding, and time available to dedicate to its development. This vast variance makes it almost silly to talk about in any other way but via one isolated example case: the one of an effect that I shall describe below!

———————— THIS IS REAL (ORIGINAL VERSION) ————————

It was the fall of 2000, probably. I was visiting my alma mater, Penn State University, from whence I had graduated a mere few months prior. Sipping the quintessential college beer of the area, I sat with my long-time friend and eventual roommate, Dave Smith (since changed to Dave Darwin), and talked about the not so distant good ol' days of writing routines together as young, foolish, college kids. We discussed magic, juggling, philosophy, and performance, and I eventually mustered up the courage to boldly try a concept that surely wouldn't work. And really, it didn't, but it was certainly worth pursuing in such a casual jam-session situation.

I sat across from Dave and gestured around the table. "What is real? What makes you so sure it is? Because our eyes, nose, or ears tell us? Does it exist first and then we sense it? Or do we imagine it and our senses then decide to 'make' it exist so we don't seem as crazy as we are?" (Side note: I had recently read a fantastic and fantastical short story/essay by the great Argentine author Jorge Luis Borges, in which the question was posed: What if the entire universe and everything we know to exist came into being only ten seconds ago? Everything we think we know, everything we sense to be real, that we "remember" having happened, is really just a concoction of our imaginations so as to quell the insanely hard-to-swallow fact that none of what we know is "real." A little "out there." A little deep. But perfect fodder for a magic trick, I think.)

At this point, I reached out with my empty right hand and mimed the action of grabbing a pen from the air. With both hands, I continued the act of uncapping the pen. I held my open, flat, left palm toward myself and took the imaginary pen to write an imaginary message across the skin of my very real palm. At its completion, I turned my left palm toward Dave and revealed that, in fact, there was a message printed in ink across the palm. When he looked back to my right hand, I was holding an actual uncapped pen. The end.

The method I concocted for that evening began by me conditioning him to see and believe that my left hand was clean of ink until the performance time. Then, perhaps a minute or two before I was ready to try the piece, I dropped both hands into my lap, where an uncapped pen was waiting. As I let him lead the conversation through some certainly animated and interesting story, I secretly wrote "This is Real" on the palm of my left hand. Then I waited. At the right (or write) moment, I said, "Let me try an idea." I then, keeping the pen in my lap, gestured/pointed forward with my left hand (without flashing the writing) and then reached forward with my right hand to pluck the invisible/imaginary pen from the air. I mimed the actions of removing the cap and placing it on the other end of the pen. Next, I "wrote" on my left palm, tracing the letters that were actually there. As I thrust my left palm forward to show the result, I casually but quickly dipped my right hand to the lap to retrieve the real pen and have it displayed by the time Dave looked back to the right hand. From this choppy, improvisational concept was born a magical premise that has haunted me as a fun and maddening thought experiment for the past fourteen years.

From there I began to work out different methods that would be more practical or at least somewhat plausible to perform. Among them were:

1. Write the phrase ahead of time, but cover it with an easily removed/wiped-away makeup.

Issue: Would have to perform this first so as not to smear the makeup, plus finding the right makeup to work proved more challenging than one might think.

2.Secretly have a small writing implement (mini marker or pen tip) to write the phrase, and then attach it or palm it when the real pen is produced.

Issue: Less clean than I'd like. Also a little more "angley", but a viable option.

3. Create a rubber stamp with the phrase written out in my handwriting, and have it somewhere (in pocket or on a belt) that I could instantly

"stamp" the message rather than write it out slowly ahead of time.

Issue: Though I was excited for this one, I never got a good enough stamp that didn't mark other parts of the hand or look somehow suspicious/incomplete. A "more clever than good" idea.

1. Change the effect so the writing does not appear on the palm of the hand, but on a blank business/index card. In this case, as with most of the others, the pen would start up the right sleeve. Take a single business card, blank both sides, and write "This is Real" on one side. For the performance, take it out and apparently display both sides via the business card paddle move generally credited to Francis Carlyle (but predating Carlyle was Douglas Dexter in 1931). In this case, the point is to casually display both sides of the card blank without making a big deal of it. Then mime the actions of producing the pen and uncapping and then writing with it. Display the card's writing as the right hand drops and retrieves the pen from the sleeve. By the time the spectator looks back to the right hand, the pen is in view, held in writing position.

Issue: While this works well, and is probably the version I've used the most, it suffers by not having quite the same organic feel that comes from writing on one's hand. That said, for those who do not like the idea of writing on their bodies, this can be a strong, viable option.

5. Use a slightly adjusted version of Theodore Deland's Fadeaway card, on which is printed (or copied) the color and design of the palm of a hand. In its basic form, it is a camouflaged card made to look as though the hand palming it is empty. In this case, one side would be flesh-toned, and the other would be black (or the color of your trousers.) Also embedded or glued to the card in some fashion would be a magnet or a shim so it could be ditched by sticking it to a magnet in the pants pocket or somewhere similar. In operation, the writing would be done ahead of time. At the time of performance, the Fadeaway Card would be palmed so that the palm could be flashed casually to the audience. The marker/pen would start up the sleeve of the right hand.

As the right hand reaches forward to grab the imaginary pen from the air, the left hand would casually drop off the card in its ditch position (or into a servante). The faux-writing act would take place, and then the left hand would turn and display the now-visible writing as the right hand unsleeves the pen. The final beat would be to turn and look at the pen, and then to look and acknowledge the audience once again.

Issue: I haven't done this yet. It was an idea that came from brainstorming with two talented and creative magician friends of mine in Philadelphia: Don Camp and Fred Siegel. Over an evening with cigars, wine, and a lot of philosophy and humor, this was a very viable (I think) option for one way of performing "This is Real." I look forward to trying it out, and to you continuing the pursuit of a method for this same effect.

The point, which I'm sure is obvious by now, is that the creative process is not a cut-and-dried path where one has a problem and then finds the solution. "This is Real" is just one example of one "trick" plot that I've played with and will likely continue to play with for the rest of my life. Once in awhile, I dig the effect out and take it off its "shelf." I reintroduce myself, making small talk of how I've progressed since last we met and how I think we may be able to work together in new and different ways. Creating new solutions for old problems keeps the ingenuity alive and fresh. I may never use most of the methods that I create for any given effect, but they may find themselves crossing over into other effects and in turn making them better. Then I'll put the piece back on its shelf (or into the act) until we feel like playing together again. For a more in-depth look at this notion of "never being satisfied" with any given method, look to the legendary creator and performer of magic, Tommy Wonder, in his two volume set, The Books of Wonder. Each solution he provides for any given effect proves markedly more impressive and appropriate than the previous one. Take the time. Hunt down the books. They will inspire you, as they inspire us all, to make our magic better. Before I leave you to the rest of the wonderful ideas that many creative friends have shared in this book, allow me to put forth the version of "This is Real" that I actually created early on and now use in certain very specific theatrical productions. Enjoy. And keep questioning everything.

I first created and performed this version of the piece for my show "Stranger than

Fiction" several years ago. It was a dark, twisted piece to begin a darker, more twisted show. I've since improved the method and streamlined the script to fit into a David Lynch themed performance piece with a burlesque dancer friend of mine. Suffice to say, it worked in a delightfully weird and wonderful way.

THIS IS REAL (MACBETH'S DAGGER)

The Premise

The performer walks out on stage with nothing. There is a single table, slightly downstage right, with a white towel, a bit damp, sitting atop it. Reaching center stage, the performer looks out to the crowd and announces, "None of this is real. You are not real. You are all mere figments of my imagination, fragments of a dream. These lights aren't real. This stage, this table, this chair isn't real!" (All of this is said while gesturing at the mentioned features. Only the chair actually does not exist, making for an extra absurd moment in the story.)

The performer looks forward, and then reaches out with his right hand as though to grab an invisible dagger from the air by its handle. "This knife isn't real. It's blade isn't sharp…it can't CUT me." On the word "cut," the performer mimes the action of slicing his hand with the blade of the knife, essentially dragging his right thumb across the left palm. The performer then turns and tilts his left palm directly to the audience, revealing a long, bloody gash along his hand. The audience then looks to the performer's right hand to discover that the knife has now appeared. The performer tables the knife and cleans his hands of the blood with the towel, and then carries on with the show.

The Details

fig. 1

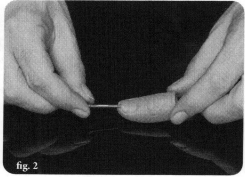
fig. 2

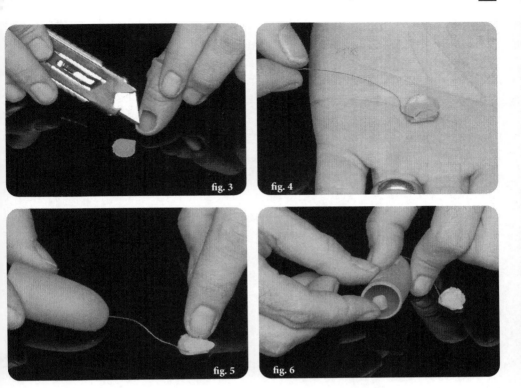

The knife that I use is a custom-made dagger that I occasionally use for other effects, including the stabbed-in-the-back finale to my show. (Well, it's sort of the same prop.) I also have an extremely strong rare-earth magnet that sits in my right rear trousers pocket. When I walk out on stage, the knife is stuck to my butt, blade pointed toward the ground, via the magnet (fig. 1).

Other props include a specially doctored thumb tip with a small hole (1/16" diameter) at the tip of the "nail" of the gaff (fig. 2). From another thumb tip, I cut out the thumbnail and epoxied the end of a thickish length of blood-red thread, about two inches long, to the underside of the nail. A little bit of magician's wax is used to adhere the extra nail to the full thumb tip (figs. 3 and 4). The length of thread is then fed through the small hole into the thumb tip (fig. 5). Another dab of magician's wax is used to plug the hole so that the thumb tip can be filled part way with stage blood and not leak out through the hole (fig. 6).

Take about a teaspoon or so (not much more) of stage blood and pour it into the thumb tip, obviously keeping it mouth-side up so as not to leak blood (fig. 7).

Make sure the blood sufficiently soaks the thread inside the tip, as that is going to help the thread stick to the palm while looking like a runny, bloody gash.

As final preparation, I coat my left palm with a thin layer of rubber cement. This, too, will assist in the sticking of the bloody thread to my palm (fig. 8).

The Performance
With knife loaded and blood-tip lodged snugly on my right thumb, I enter the stage and find my way to center. Angles are sensitive, as I don't want to flash the knife prematurely. Facing the audience, I pause theatrically, staring at them curiously, and then begin the script. The actions are fairly easy to imagine: The mimed action of grabbing the knife happens when I say, "This knife isn't real." I then bring the thumb tip to the leftmost side of my left palm, using the left thumb to "pop off" the fake nail and to grip it essentially in thumb palm as I drag the right thumb tip along the palm. Doing so drags the bloody string out and along the palm to form a rather convincing gash from even a short distance away (fig. 9). As the thumb tip clears the bottom edge of the palm, I

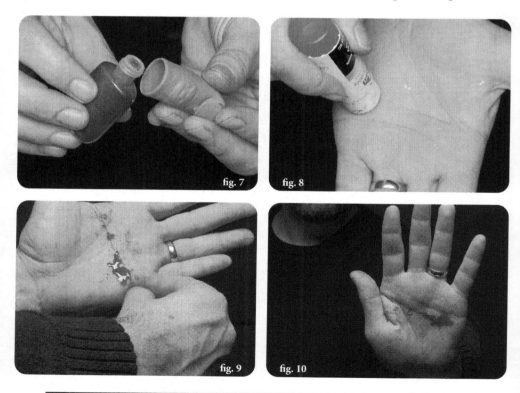

fig. 7

fig. 8

fig. 9

fig. 10

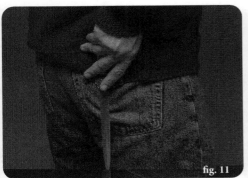

fig. 11

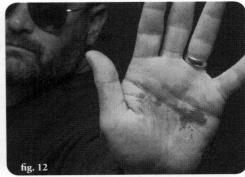

fig. 12

fig. 13

let the right hand drop to the side. The next combination of actions happens simultaneously: I thrust the left palm forward and angled toward the audience so they can see the newly formed "gash" (fig. 10). Meanwhile, the right hand continues its "dropping" journey to swoop around, grab the knife handle (fig. 11), and continue backward and out to the right as I rotate my whole body slightly to the left (fig. 12). It's almost a smooth dance-like move from start to finish so as to make the appearance of the knife all the more startling when it is finally discovered (fig. 13). I then table the knife, clean my hand, and move along.

The point of putting this in print is not so much so that you, my friends, can go and perform it. Certainly, as it's in print here, I can't stop you. But I'd rather you look at this from an inspirational standpoint rather than a tutorial on how to do something that, frankly, will very likely not work for you or your stage personality. Instead, look at the routine ideas you have and the pieces you've done and have a conversation with them. See who they are, what they want, and what the two of you can accomplish together with just a little ingenuity and a fair amount of work. You'll create wonderful experiences for your audiences, and just may surprise yourself. For real.

Greasy Pretzel Fingers

Effect

The magician crumbles up a few knotted pretzels in his empty hand to demonstrate a new "gambling cheating move". The pretzel grease is utilized as a way to make an impromptu "slick card". After a failed attempt, the rest of the pretzels that were left over are crushed in the fist. When the hand is opened, the crumbs that are left over are shown to reveal the name of the previously selected "slick" card.

Needed

A handful of small, knotted pretzels, a napkin, and a deck of playing cards.

Preparation

While at a bar, party, funeral, or some other occasion where a big bowl of knotted pretzels may be present, grab a hold of a few of them and excuse yourself to the bathroom or any other private place. While you are in there, you will break one of the pretzels into a "9" shape. You will break another pretzel into a "heart" shape (fig. 1). There is really no intricate technique to this and it will require practice to get it down smoothly. I find it best to moisten the areas that you are about to break with your tongue. This will help prevent the pretzel from shattering into a million little pieces while breaking it apart. After the pretzel has been moistened, pick away at the area with your fingernail until you get the desired shape. If you should accidentally break the pretzel in a way that is not desired, start over using one of the extra pretzels that you brought with you. If somebody should ask you why you are bringing pretzels into the bathroom, tell them, "I might get hungry. I plan on being in there for a loooong time." There should be no more questions.

In order to break the "9", look at the pretzel as if it were made up of two distinct parts. On the left side, there is a reversed "9" shape, and on the right side, there is a regular "9" shape. You need to separate this pretzel directly down the middle (fig. 2). Once this has been accomplished, dispose of the reversed "9". Trim up the end of the stem that hangs down from the loop. You should now have a good looking "9" (fig. 3).

In order to break the "heart", look at the pretzel as if it were made up of two parts as well; they are an upside down "Y" shape that is surrounded by a "heart" shape. Using the same technique to break apart the pretzel as before, carefully remove the inner "Y" shape (fig. 4). Dispose of the "Y" piece. This will leave you with a very nice looking "heart" shape. Take note that this "Y" removal is probably the hardest part of this entire routine. Stay at it and pick away in small pieces. With enough practice, you can easily set up these pretzels in a couple of minutes with no problem at all.

These prepared pieces are held in left-hand finger palm. Place the Nine of Hearts face down on top of the face-down deck. Place the deck of cards in your right-hand pocket and you are ready to go.

fig. 1   fig. 2

fig. 3   fig. 4

Performance

Approach a table that has a bowl of pretzels on it. Having people at that table makes it even more entertaining.

> *"You know the old expression 'Cheaters never win and winners never cheat'? I don't know if I totally agree with that. I think what they meant to say was 'If you're going to cheat, be a winner about it.' Cheat with some style!!"*

Reach into your right-hand pocket to retrieve the deck and place it face down, directly on top of the finger-palmed pretzels in your left hand. Your left hand will be loosely holding the deck above the prepared pretzels. Do not press down on top of the deck too hard with your left thumb, as you may accidentally break the pretzel pieces.

> *"I'd like to show you an example of how you can use everyday, ordinary items to help you cheat in almost any situation."*

Point to the bowl of pretzels and ask the spectator to pick up a small handful of them. Roughly four or five will do. Instruct them to rub their fingers all over the pretzels in order to get a good layer of "grease" on them.

> *"This is the latest in junk-food-cheating technological advances. I'm going to teach you how to cut to any card you want, just by using a few of these pretzels here. Intrigued? I knew that you would be. The first thing you need to do is load up your fingers with something greasy. These pretzels will do the trick. Don't be shy. Get a good layer of grease all over your fingertips."*

Rub the back of the top card of the deck with your right index finger, demonstrating to the spectator exactly how you are going to want a selected card to be marked later.

> *"You are going to mark the back of a randomly selected card with a big blotch of pretzel grease. Now, this grease will be invisible to the naked eye, but because of its slippery nature, you will be able to cut to it anytime you want."*

You are going to force the spectator to select the Nine of Hearts. To do this, you will be utilizing the Cut Deeper Force, a beautiful move often attributed to Ed Balducci, but in fact, was originally published in Sam Mayer's "Another Do as I Do", in the *Sphinx, Vol. 45 No. 5, July 1946*)." This version of the force justifies the necessity of cutting the deck twice. It is accomplished in two parts. The first part is performed by the magician, as if he is instructing the spectator on what he wants them to do next. Demonstrate this by cutting off approximately one-third of the deck, turning it face up, and then depositing it face up on top of the deck (fig. 5). Note that during the entire cutting/turnover procedure, the cards are gripped solely by the fingertips, as they hold the cards by their ends.

"What I would like you to do is cut about a third of the cards off of the deck, turn them over, and drop them face up on top of the deck, but be careful not to touch the backs of the cards or you might accidentally grease the wrong one. Try and hold them by their ends, just like this, OK?"

Once the cards have been replaced face up on top of the deck, instruct the spectator to perform the entire cutting/turnover process for themselves, but as an afterthought, instruct the spectator to cut off about half of the deck before turning it over (fig. 6).

"So, go ahead and cut off about…oh, I don't know…do about the half of the deck this time. Remember to hold the cards by the ends. Perfect. Now turn them over. Excellent."

To complete the force, instruct the spectator to remove all of the face-up

fig. 5

fig. 6

cards until they reach the first face-down card (fig. 7). This will be the Nine of Hearts, but the spectator will think that this was a randomly cut-to card.

> *"Now go ahead and gently brush off all of the face-up cards until you reach the first face-down card. We'll use that one as our selected card."*

Have the spectator remove the selected card and remember it. Once they have committed it to memory, instruct the spectator to rub their "greased up" fingers all over the back of the card. Get them to have some fun with this. Remember, grease is the word! Once that has been done, put the selected card back onto the face-down deck. Place the brushed-off face-up cards back onto the deck, face down. You have just lost their selected card into the center of the pack.

> *"Go ahead and remember that card. Got it? Good. Now, go ahead and rub your greasy fingers all over the back of it. Get it good and grimy. Fantastic. Feels good, doesn't it? Now put it back into the center of the pack and put those cards back on top of it. Just like a born cheater."*

Explain that they are going to try and cut directly to their greased-up card all on their own. Have them cut off about half of the pack, turn it over, and drop it on the deck, just as they did before. They need only do this cutting/turnover procedure one time, as opposed to doing it twice, as in the Cut-Deeper force. In this case, you actually want the spectator to miss the card. Have them remove the face-up cards, stopping at the first face-down card that they see.

fig. 7

> *"Now, it's time to put your pretzel fingers to the test. Go ahead and try and cut directly to your card. It takes a light touch. Remember, hold them by their edges when you cut them. Turn them over, drop them on the deck, and then brush away those face-up cards. Let's take a look at what card you cut to. Was that your card?"*

Thumb over the card and turn it over for the big revelation. They will state that it is not theirs, unless they happened to actually cut to the greased-up, selected card. If this happens, celebrate this unlikely miracle and go home with a big greasy smile on your face. More likely than not, they will have missed. Turn the card face down and put it on top of the pack.

> *"No. That wasn't it, huh? Well, don't feel bad. It does take a light touch, and besides, maybe you weren't using enough grease."*

Ask the spectator to hand you all of the pretzels that they removed at the beginning of the demonstration. Have them place these pretzels onto your outstretched right hand, which should now be held over a napkin, so that you do not make a giant mess. Make sure that your right palm is seen to be completely empty before taking these pieces.

> *"Whenever I run into trouble with this technique, I usually just double or triple the amount of grease I had originally used. Hand me all of those pretzels, if you don't mind. This could get kind of messy."*

Make a tight fist with your right hand. Crumble the pretzels into as many small pieces as you can make with this one hand. Keep rolling them around and crushing them, but be sure not to open up your right hand at all during this process.

> *"What you have to do is get the pretzel grease way deep down into your pores, like this. There, that feels better."*

fig. 8   fig. 9

Hold your right fist so that the thumbhole is pointing upward. Relax your right hand just enough to let a thin stream of crumbs begin to pour out of the bottom of the fist (fig. 8). A small circular motion of the right fist helps to ensure that an even stream of crumb pieces falls onto the napkin.

"Isn't that pretty? Pretty greasy is more like it. By the way, what was your selected card?"

Allow all of the crumb pieces to pour out from the bottom of the fist, but remember to keep your right fist closed during the release of these pieces (fig. 9). Once they have all fallen out, shake your right fist as if there is still something inside of it.

"The Nine of Hearts? Hmmmm. Well, that feels about right."

You are going to make it appear as if the "Nine of Hearts" pretzel pieces were left inside of the right-hand fist after all of the leftover crumbs have been poured out. To do this, you will execute a sneaky version of the time honored Han Ping Chien move (*The Han Ping Chien Coin Trick* by Ladson Butler, 1917). In preparation for this move, ask the spectator to cup their hands together and to hold them above the napkin. Allow your left hand and its pack of cards to hover above their outstretched hands. Shake your right fist one last time to signify that there "is something left in there".

"Cup your hands together and hold them over the napkin. Perfect. Now, if my touch is right and I have used enough grease, we may get lucky. Actually, instead of cutting to the card, let me show you something even cooler. I have a few crumbs left over in my hand. Let's see what they look like, shall we?"

Perform the Han Ping Chien move by turning your right fist palm down, opening it up in the process, and making a tossing motion with it toward their cupped hands. At the same time this is being done, move the left hand sharply to the left. The laws of physics will keep the prepared pretzel pieces suspended in mid-air momentarily, as the left hand moves out of the way. The pieces should ricochet lightly off of the right-hand fingertips before falling into the spectator's hands (fig. 10). It

fig. 10   fig. 11

will appear exactly as if the pieces were tossed from the right fist into the spectator's cupped hands. Using your right hand, dramatically arrange the two pieces that have been dumped into their cupped hands into "The Nine of Hearts" (fig. 11).

"Check it out!! The Nine of Hearts. Wow! Isn't that amazing? You see? That… is how you cheat like a winner; a greasy winner, but a winner none the less!!"

Oh Yeah...

Give this one a try. It's a perfect trick for certain social gatherings. I believe that everybody is interested in cheating techniques, so there is a very nice presentation hook built in. I enjoy the thinking behind the rationale for having to turn over the cards twice during the Cut Deeper Force. Utilizing the first turnover as an instructional opportunity takes the heat off of having to cut the deck twice. Also, don't be afraid of the Han Ping Chien move from under the deck. It is not difficult to do at all. Finally, remember to exercise a little bit of care when dealing with the pretzels. The last thing you want to have happen is for one of your finale pretzel pieces to break during the routine.

The 80's Called... They Want Their Magic Book Back

Effect
An ordinary card case defies gravity as it levitates off of an ordinary deck of cards with no wires, magnets, or remote control helicopters used whatsoever. This is definitely an impromptu miracle worth "bragging about".

Needed
A deck of cards and a card case.

Preparation
None.

Performance
Begin with the deck inside the card box. You will want to be situated directly across from the spectator, one on one, face to face, mano a mano, with both of you looking down at the cards from above.

> *"Let me ask you a question. Is it better to know a little about a lot or a lot about a little? I'm more of a 'little about a lot' kind of guy. Knowing a lot about a little implies that one is an expert in a specific field. The only thing I am an expert on is non-expertise."*

Remove the deck from the box and give the cards to the spectator to look over.

> *"Right now, I'd like your expertise on these playing cards. Completely normal, right?"*

Take the deck back from the spectator and hold it in left-hand dealer's grip as the right hand gives the spectator the card case to explore as well.

> *"And the card case is ordinary as well, correct?"*

While the case is being examined, spread over approximately fifteen cards or so between the hands.

You are going to be culling, or secretly pulling a card underneath the right hand's spread, so it ends up perpendicular to the rest of the cards. To do this, the tip of your right index finger contacts the edge of the upper right corner of the card to be culled; in this instance, the card approximately fifteenth from the top as the rest of the right fingers contact the face of that card (fig. 1, from beneath). The tip of your left thumb lies across the deck, contacting only the left edge of the card directly above the card to be culled (fig. 2). Your right fingers pull their card slightly downward and to the right, kind of like the Nike "swoosh" symbol, by bending inward toward the palm. This will cause the card to pivot counter-clockwise around the right index finger, which is acting as a fulcrum, ending up perpendicular to the right-hand cards above it (fig.

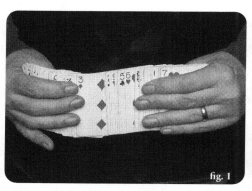

fig. 1

fig. 2

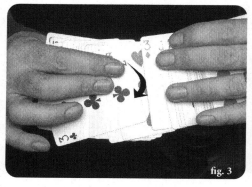

fig. 3

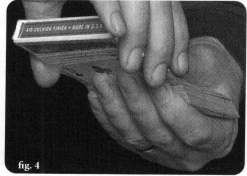

fig. 4

3). Note that the spread of cards is never broken apart during this move.

> *"Well, 'hot air' or not, it has served me pretty well in life. Because if there is one thing that I know about, it's life. Oh, the stories I can tell you. I took a sociology class in school once, so of course, I'm a qualified expert."*

Transfer the entire spread back to the left hand, extending your left thumb to the right so that it can clamp down on the back of the top card of the spread, holding the cards in place.

> *"See what I did there? That's some of that 'hot air' that we were talking about."*

Your right hand is now free to pick up the card case from above in overhand grip and place it side-jogged to the right of the top card of the spread. The right hand maintains its overhand grip on the case as both hands tilt slightly to the left, elevating the right ends of the cards (fig. 4). The left thumb releases its grip just enough to allow gravity to close the spread. Once the cards hit the fork of the left hand, re-grip the deck with your left thumb.

> *"Because if there is one thing that I know about, it's hot air."*

The card case is now obscuring the protruding card from view. Push your left fingers to the right until they have straightened out completely,

fig. 5

fig. 6

further extending the card from the deck (fig. 5). Be careful not to extend the card past the right edge of the card case. Push up the right end of the protruding card with the right middle and ring fingers so that the card is bending at a ninety-degree angle. This will raise the card case in your right hand just a little bit, as it now is sitting on top of the card (fig. 6, from behind).

"I read a book on hot-air ballooning last week..."

While keeping the card case in contact with the top edge of the protruding card, slowly lower the case down and to the left, until it is directly over the cards in the left hand. This action folds the card loosely in half (with a block of cards inside of it) under the card box. You do not want to crease this folded card. It should be in a loose backward letter "C" shape (fig. 7).

"...sooooo, I think I know what I'm talking about."

The situation should be as follows: approximately fourteen cards or so are inside of the loosely folded protruding card, which itself is trapped between the remainder of the deck and the underside of the card case.

Once the card box is in position over the deck, hold the front of the case between your thumb and first two fingers of your left hand, with the thumb holding the outer left corner and the index and middle fingers pinching the outer right corner. The side of the case nearest you is locked

fig. 7

fig. 8

in position by the ball of the left thumb and the left ring finger (fig. 8).

"Look, I'll prove it to you."

While keeping the front edge of the case and deck pressed together, so there are no visible breaks or gaps, raise the card case up to your mouth with both hands and blow into the flap-side of the box as if you were inflating a balloon.

"I'll fill the card case up with some of this 'hot air' that I've been blowing around."

Remove your right hand as you lower the left hand back down so that both you and the spectator are looking down at the top of the case. Press your right index finger down onto the center of the front of the case as you release the left-hand grip, allowing the cards and the case to lie directly on your flattened palm. The right index finger is now the only thing keeping the case from popping off of the deck.

"Since air expands as it heats, it becomes lighter than the air around it..."

To make the case do its floating thing, slowly raise your right hand up and to the right, while keeping the index finger firmly in contact with the case. There are some balance issues to contend with as you make the case float, but the knack is absolutely acquired with just a little bit of practice. Just try to keep your index finger directly in line with the edge of the folded card as it unbends (fig. 9). If your index finger falls on either side of the edge of the card below the case, you will have difficulties. When looking down from above, the illusion that the card box is floating two to three inches above the cards is perfect.

fig. 9

> *"...causing it to float up and away. It's science. And I know all about science because I used to watch Bill Nye, The Science Guy, every day, so I'm kind of an authority on the topic."*

Reverse these actions in order to bring the case safely back down to the deck in the left hand. Once the case touches down on the cards, re-grip everything as you did before with the left thumb and fingers. This will keep the case locked in place, as your right hand resumes its overhand grip on the case as well in preparation to blow into the card case again.

> *"That's pretty cool, isn't it? Let's try a big one!"*

Both hands are brought up toward the mouth in order to "inflate" it one more time. Blow a very big breath into the case after you say the following in a voice as if you were holding smoke in your lungs:

> *"I'm college educated, with two majors, three minors, and a GPA of 3.6, but I really don't mean to brag."*

Blow another big breath into the case after holding it in, saying:

> *"I should go on the game show Jeopardy because I can't remember the last time I missed a question while watching at home."*

Take a really deep breath and, before exhaling out all of your air into the card case with one last over-exaggerated breath, say the following line:

fig. 10

fig. 11

> *"I'm street smart, worldly wise, and I have very strong opinions, which are half right at least more than half of the time."*

Lower the case and the deck back down to their original position. I like to start to shake and twitch my left hand, as if I were trying to hold something in place before it explodes out of my hand. Bring your palm-down right hand about three inches above the case and, when you have "built up enough pressure", simply release the left hand's grip. The case will pop off of the deck very fast and smack into the outstretched right hand, which stops the case from shooting all of the way off of the bent card (fig. 10). This is a great moment.

> *"Wow, that was a lot. I'm kind of light-headed now. The case definitely feels likes it's going to pop any second. Boom!!! There it goes!"*

Use your right hand to slowly push the case back down onto the cards in the left hand. Once the case has touched back down onto the cards, re-grip it one last time between the left thumb and fingers, as your right hand resumes its overhand grip on it as well. By momentarily lifting up the right side of the case a bit, the face-up side of the bent card will unfold to the right and protrude out from the deck again.

> *"When using 'hot air', you must be very careful, because when you heat up gases, you run the risk of going up in flames if you push it too far."*

You will right this protruding card by contacting its upper right corner from underneath with the left fingers. Use these fingers to push the protruding card toward your body, clockwise, where it gets righted back into the deck (fig. 11). This action is covered as the right hand revolves everything in the left hand, end for end, in a 180-degree squaring action.

> *"I know a lot about flames because we used to live close to the fire department when I was growing up, so I'm kind of like an honorary Fire Marshal."*

Repeat this "squaring circle" one more time, to ensure that the larger motion of revolving the pack has sufficiently hidden the smaller action of righting the protruding card into the rest of the deck. Give the pack a nice pressure fan or card spring in order to take the bend out of the card and then get out of town quickly before someone smacks you upside your bragging head.

"'Hot Air'. Use it wisely."

Oh Yeah…

Let's discuss the obvious. You are definitely left with one seriously warped card afterward, and I will be the first to admit that it doesn't always come out so easy when doing a pressure fan or card spring. If killing a card in the name of entertainment offends you, you could certainly start off the routine with a Joker or some other extra card that you hate and wouldn't mind harming on top of the deck. If you Slip Cut that card about fifteen cards down and hold a pinky break above it, you could then just spread to the break and resume with the cull. I have also played with the idea of using the bent card as part of a bend-transposition effect. Force the bent card with a face-down riffle force, being careful not to reveal its bent condition. Cut it to the center of the deck and give it to the spectator to hold on to tightly as you then take one indifferent card for yourself. Essentially, you would put an "impossible" bend into the card, something that looks far worse than it really it is. You can give a card a severe-looking crimp that simply comes out when bent the other way. The average spectator does not know how easy or hard that action is. After making the bend vanish from the card, the spectator finds that the bend has now jumped onto a selected card inside of the deck that is in their very hands. Maybe something like that?

SLOPPY SPECTATOR

Steve Mayhew

Effect
In an effort to overcome sheer laziness, the spectator and the magician share the demanding responsibility of shuffling a complete deck of cards in a crazy weird way: by mixing their cards into a face-up/face-down mess. Both then share the equally demanding task of righting the entire deck face down, with the exception of four face-up Aces that are now magically chilling in the center.

Needed
A deck of your favorite playing cards.

Preparation
Begin with the four Aces (or any four of a kind, for that matter) on the bottom of the face-down deck.

Performance
Casually spread the cards from hand to hand, showing that all the cards are face down without actually mentioning it aloud.

"I've been doing magic for a very long time, and sometimes I wonder just how many times I've actually shuffled a deck of cards."

Give the deck a few shuffles, while retaining the Aces on the bottom.

"Let's say a conservative average of twenty shuffles a day, 365 days a year, for thirty years. That's 219,000 shuffles!"

Stop shuffling, look at the deck with feigned disgust, and then square up the cards and hold them in left-hand dealer's grip.

"I think I just might be done. I truly don't have the heart to do it alone. You can call me, but you know what I always say. "There's no 'i' in laziness."

Suddenly, realize the error of your spelling ways, if the spectator doesn't do it first for you.

Extend the deck to the spectator, asking them to cut off half of the cards for themselves.

In a moment, you are going to guide the spectator through the process of a terrific yet simulated face-up/face-down mix entitled the Slop Shuffle by Sid Lorraine. This deceptive and easy-to-execute shuffle was first published in *Subtle Problems You Will Do* by Stewart Judah and John Braun (1946). It's so easy to do that a spectator, if properly guided through the procedure, could actually perform the shuffle for themselves. Really, what could be better than a move designed to fool the spectator that is actually performed in their very own "sloppy" hands?

Let's get the logistics out of the way. If you and the spectator are both right-handed (or both left-handed), stand side by side with them. If one of you is right-handed and the other left, stand facing the spectator so they can mirror your actions easily. Standing in these positions goes a long way to help ensure that the spectator can follow your hand actions as easily as possible. We will assume that both you and the spectator are right-handed individuals, for purposes of explanation.

Instruct the spectator to follow your movements exactly as you thumb off one card from the top of the pack, taking it in between the fingers and thumb of the other hand.

Replace your cards back onto your respective packs, and then demonstrate how to use the left thumb to push off multiple cards, three or four at a time, and then take them in between the fingers and thumb of the right hand.

> *"Very good. I can see you've got skills. But can you do it with... three cards at a time?"*

In a slightly embarrassed way, realize that the spectator is handling this dealing procedure with ease.

> *"OK, I see you've got that one too, huh?"*

As you continue spreading the cards from hand to hand in small batches of three or four cards at a time, in-jog the fourth card from the bottom of the deck (fig. 1).

> *"This one took me a long time to master. Maybe you are a natural. Maybe it's just beginner's luck. Since you are challenging my honor like this, let's try something a little bit more difficult."*

As you square the pack into your dealing hand, push down on the in-jogged card with the thumb of the other hand so that you can catch a left-pinky break above the four Aces on the bottom of the pack.

Now, on to the Slop Shuffle. Instruct the spectator to carefully follow and copy your movements as you again use your left thumb to push over

fig. 1   fig. 2

a small group of three or four cards. Take these cards into your palm-up right hand.

"We are going to start off slowly. Push off a few cards into your other hand…"

Next, demonstrate to the spectator that you now want them to turn the right hand palm down as the left thumb pushes another small batch of cards over to the right (fig. 2).

"…and turn these over so that your hand is palm down. Good job!"

Your right hand sloppily adds its face-up cards on top of the new group of cards that are being pushed over, where the right hand then re-grips both batches (fig. 3).

"Now, two hands at once. Push over these cards with the left thumb and then smack those cards in the right hand down on top of the ones in the left."

The right hand then turns palm up and adds its cards on top of yet another small batch of cards being pushed over by the left thumb (fig. 4).

"Turn your hand palm up again and plop those cards on top of these in the left."

Instruct the spectator to focus their energy and to look you directly in

fig. 3   fig. 4

the eyes while they continue this messy procedure of mixing face-up and face-down cards. They are to do this until they have pushed all of the cards over into the right hand. I elect to have the spectator look me in the eye while shuffling for two reasons: The first being that we are testing their concentration skills, and by locking eyes, a "better connection" can be made; The second and real reason is that it provides just a little extra insurance for anybody that may be concentrating a little too hard on their shuffling and is somehow able to put together that they are not really mixing the cards as you have stated they are.

> *"Good. But now, look me square in the eyes while we finish the rest of them. I think we are making a connection. Well, whatever it is, it felt good."*

Continue your shuffle while locking eyeballs with the spectator.

> *"Just put these on those and those under these, next to those, under these...on top of those..."*

Wrap up your messy shuffle in the same manner as the spectator is doing, but when you get to your four face-down Aces on the bottom of your deck, which are separated by the pinky break, simply add them to the top of the right-hand cards (fig. 5). The fact that the top cards of your half are face down and the spectator's are face up only adds to the illusion that the cards are really mixed up.

> *"...and those go next to these, and finally, these go on top of those."*

fig. 5

Here's a quick status check: From the top down, the spectator's cards run half face-up, followed by half face-down. Your cards run in the same order, with the exception of the four face-down Aces which are on top of everything.

Get a left-pinky break between the back-to-back cards that are in the middle of your packet, which should be fairly easy because of the natural bow in the deck. Take the spectator's cards and insert them into the break. This leaves you with the four Aces on top, followed by half of the deck face up, and then the remaining half of the deck face down.

Wait for the spectator to respond to the question, and no matter what they say, answer with a resounding:

I like to give the deck the following display. Transfer the pack to right-hand Biddle Grip, with the forefinger curled down on top off the deck. Your left hand still remains in the picture by remaining palm up underneath the deck (fig. 6). Riffle off of the bottom quarter of the pack with the right thumb, where a face-down card will show, and then catch a left-pinky break above it. Continue riffling up with the right thumb until you get to a face-up card. At this point, catch a left ring-finger break above it. With your right hand, lift up all of the cards above the ring-finger break in Biddle Grip and side-jog them to the right. Next, lift up all of the cards above the pinky break and side-jog all of them to the right as well. Display this three-leveled deck in left-hand

fig. 6   fig. 7

dealing position, with the left thumb clamped down across the top of everything (fig. 7).

"Actually, don't you think it would be even more amazing if we were totally in sync with each other..."

Square up the cards into the left hand, and then from above, use the right hand to cut to any face-up card in the upper half of the deck.

"...and we both ended up with the same number of face-up cards?"

Replace the cards and then repeat the cut, but this time, cut to any face-down card in the lower half.

"Or even the same number of face-down cards?"

As the spectator answers the question, cut one more time to a face-up card in the upper half. This cutting procedure is a fairly standard way to show multiple face-up/face-down cards.

"Me, too! In fact, I think it would be utterly incredible."

Next, use that natural bow in the deck, or you can just riffle up the back of the cards with your right thumb in order to find the spot in the deck where two cards are back to back. Separate the deck at that point by using the right hand to lift the cards from above in Biddle Grip. Rotate the right hand palm

fig. 8

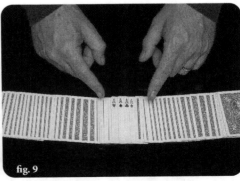

fig. 9

up to show a face-down card on top of each half (fig. 8).

> *"Don't you think it would be crazy if we both not only ended up with the same exact number of face-up cards..."*

Slide the cards in the left hand underneath the cards being held in the palm-up right hand.

> *"...but what if after all of that shuffling, all of our face-up cards were made up of the exact same number of red cards and black cards?"*

Wait for the spectator to answer the question and then reply:

> *"Me too!! But in fact, that is exactly the situation we have here. The same number of face-up cards, the same number of red/black cards, and in fact..."*

Square up everything and then use whatever magic gesture in your arsenal that gives you the most credibility with the street-magic kids out there.

> *"...the same cards altogether. You see, you found yourself a red Ace AND a black Ace!"*

Spread the deck to reveal that all of the cards are now facing the same direction, face down, except for the four Aces, which are now magically face up in the middle of everything (fig. 9).

> *"And, somehow, so did I! If that ain't a connection, I don't what it is."*

Sometimes it pays to get a little sloppy.

Oh Yeah...

There are other routines out there that utilize the Slop Shuffle in order to produce a Triumph-style effect. Jay Sankey, Jerry Andrus, Steve Beam, Harvey Cohen, Shigeo Takagi, and a host of others are just some of the greats that have published some great sloppy Triumphs. So, why another? Well, Steve has really hit upon something quite interesting. Why not let the spectator stop spectating? Get them involved in the mix by teaching them to do the Slop Shuffle for themselves. I admit that I was slightly skeptical of this before trying it out. I used to feel guilty doing the Slop Shuffle for myself. I could only imagine the agony of putting it in the spectator's hands. But I will tell you this: it has never failed me and that is the simple and sloppy truth.

Effect

A guitar pick is thrown into a pack of pasteboards, finding a selected playing card like the real-life rock-and-roll star you always wanted to be.

Needed

A deck of cards, some transparent tape, and two matching guitar picks. Attach one of the guitar picks to the front end of a face-down card. The pick should be taped so that it is lying horizontally on its side. The best picks to use for this effect are jazz picks. These measure 25 mm x 23 mm, which is about the size of a penny (fig. 1). Also you will want to get the heaviest pick available, with a thickness of at least 1.25 mm.

Preparation

Tear off a small piece of tape, roughly half an inch or so, and use it to attach the pick to the card. It should be overlapping for half of its length past the card's front edge (fig. 2). Smooth out any bubbles or creases on the taped pick (fig. 3). When the taped pick is as smooth as it can be, give it a test run by folding the pick backward, using the tape as a hinge, and then letting it spring back up into position. If all is good in the neighborhood, fold the taped pick back down onto the back of the card and then place this card onto the bottom of the pack. Put the deck into the case so that the taped end is nearest the case's opening. Place the cased deck and the duplicate pick into your right pocket and let's go ahead and rock this thing.

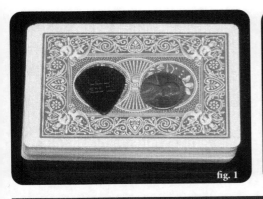

fig. 1

fig. 2

Performance

Demonstrate some of your very best "air-guitar" skills as you talk. Go for broke. You know you have it inside of it you, so let it rip.

"I'm sure that you have heard of 'air guitar' before. Young kids all over the rock-and-roll world develop their guitar shredding skills with a little bit of this and a little bit of that."

Put away your imaginary air guitar and take out an imaginary deck of cards. With the same "rock-and-roll" bravado as you did with the air guitar, pantomime doing a series of flashy, over-the-top cuts and shuffles as you are explaining "air cardistry". Throw in some pretend card fans and spring flourishes, as well as the standard finger-flicking positions that occur during these fancy-dandy cardistry routines.

"But what about the magic kids out there? Well, somewhere in the world, there is a kid tearing it up in the mirror with own flashy brand of 'air cardistry'. He can do all the tricky moves, shuffles, cuts, and things you've never even dreamed of with ease, and look good doing it, too".

Put away your imaginary deck of cards. If you really nailed your routine, you might want to consider giving the imaginary deck to a lovely audience member, but only do so if you really, really crushed that routine, or if they are really, really good looking.

"'Air Cardistry'. You'll see. It'll be sweeping the nation in no time. But until that amazing day arrives…"

fig. 3

fig. 4

As you deliver the next line, gesture with each open hand as you say "magic" and "rock and roll". After that visual display, clap both open palms together when you say the word "smash". Basically, it's "magic" on the right, "rock and roll" on the left...and then you smash 'em both together.

> *"I have figured out a way to take the mystery of magic and the raw power of rock and roll and smash them together into something really awesome."*

Reach into your pocket and bring out the guitar pick, displaying it on your right palm for everybody to see.

> *"Here is my lucky guitar pick. I caught this when I was front row at my 16th Barry Manilow concert. What can I say? I'm a Fanilow."*

Hand the pick to the spectator and then take the deck out of your pocket. Remove the cards from the case and hold them in left-hand dealer's position, with the taped end of the bottom card closest to you (fig. 4). Note that in the illustration, the taped card is separated from the deck strictly for explanation purposes. The deck should remain flat on top of the taped card, which itself is lying flat upon your palm in left-hand dealer's grip. Exercise a little bit of caution when doing this to prevent the taped gimmick from accidentally snagging and breaking free as you remove it from the case. Also, be aware of your angles on your right side. There is an opportunity to flash since the pick is creating a little gap at the back of the deck. Table the case or put it away into your pocket.

> *"Since then, every time I use it, real magic happens. I'll show you what I mean."*

Spread the deck between your hands and invite the spectator to touch the back of a card with your guitar pick.

> *"Take my lucky pick and 'pick a card'. Use the guitar pick to just touch the back of any card that you like."*

Break the spread at the card they "picked" and use the right-hand cards to flip the selected card, which in our case will be The Two of Hearts, face up onto the left-hand half of the pack (fig. 5).

Extend your left hand forward and have the spectator remove their selected card. Replace the right-hand cards underneath the rest of the cards in the left hand and square them up, holding them in dealer's grip. The taped guitar pick is now sandwiched in the middle of the deck, at its rear (fig. 6). Instruct them to now "pick" their card by holding the card like a guitar and picking away at it… like an "air guitar-card god". Encourage them to get those fingers flying up and down that card.

fig. 5   fig. 6

*"Here's your chance to be a rock star. I want you to play your selection like a
guitar. Show us what you got. C'mon, get Eddie Van Halen all over that card."*

When the spectator gets done with their "air-guitar-card" solo, throw up your best set of rock-and-roll devil horns or a simple thumbs-up gesture to congratulate them on a job well done.

*"Rock and roll!!! I just want you to know that was truly amazing. You are
definitely a tough act to follow, but I think I'm ready for the encore."*

Take the card back from the spectator and hold it face down in the right hand, with the thumb on top and your index and middle fingers beneath. Insert the selection into the gap directly above the taped guitar pick at the rear of the deck. To prevent the card from accidentally dislodging the taped pick as it is being put into the deck, use the selection to lift the upper block just a little bit while

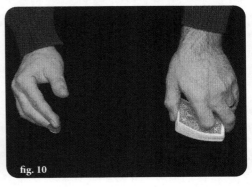

inserting the selection (fig. 7, from behind). Again, this break in the photograph is exaggerated for purposes of clarity. From the front, it should simply look as if you have just inserted the selection into the middle of the deck, which, in fact, is exactly what you just did.

> *"Your selected card goes back into the center of the deck. Now, I've been known to shred a little bit myself, but in a different way."*

Temporarily grab ahold of the deck with the right hand, thumb above and fingers below. Transfer the deck to left-hand Biddle Grip, with the left thumb closest to you (fig. 8). Re-adjust your left index finger so that the back of its first joint is contacting the top card, prepared to flex the cards backward as if you were doing a riffle shuffle (fig. 9). Take the guitar pick back from the spectator and hold it in between the thumb and first two fingers of the right hand, displaying it clearly.

> *"Check this out!!! Watch the guitar pick. Watch the cards."*

Rest the backs of the left fingertips on the table, while continuing to hold the deck from above in riffle-shuffle position. Turn the left hand so that the thumb and the taped-back pick are pointing toward your right hand, which is now winding up to apparently toss the pick into the deck (fig. 10).

> *"Watch the guitar pick 'pick' your card...just like a real rock star."*

You are now going to make it appear as if you just threw the pick directly into the pack, right next to the selected card. I have to tell you, performing the following actions simply makes me smile because it is just so fun to do.

You will use the first two fingers of your right hand to carry the pick into thumb palm as the entire hand winds-up, ready to throw (fig. 11). This wind-up provides perfect cover for the smaller action of thumb palming the pick (fig. 12). As soon as the right hand reaches the apex of its wind-up, your left hand begins to riffle its cards off of the left thumb. As the right hand pantomimes tossing the pick toward the deck, the left hand slowly riffles its

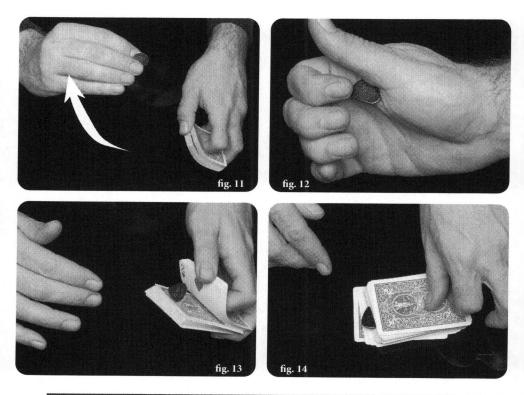

fig. 11   fig. 12

fig. 13   fig. 14

cards until the taped pick unfolds and pops out of the pack (fig. 13). The key is to riffle the left-hand cards at a speed that is slow enough, but not too slow. When the riffle is done at the proper speed, it allows for enough space to occur between the falling cards, allowing the pick to pop out into view (fig. 14). If you are having any difficulties making the pick pop out of the deck, it is likely due to the cards riffling too fast and too close together, preventing the appropriate amount of "poppage" from happening. When you get the timing right, it is an absolutely perfect illusion, and man, does it look sweet!

"The pick has actually flown straight into the deck..."

Cradle the deck from above with the left hand and then turn it so that the pick is pointing directly at the spectator. While the left hand is busy doing this, allow the thumb-palmed pick in the right hand to drop into finger palm. Pick up the deck up from above with the left hand and place it into right-hand dealer's grip, directly on top of the finger-palmed pick (fig. 15).

"...slicing its way right underneath one card."

The left hand lifts off all of the cards above the taped pick in Biddle Grip position and then turns palm up to display the Two of Hearts (fig. 16). Notice that as the left hand turns palm up, the right thumb extends over to "pin the pick in place" on top of the right-hand cards, but really, its main objective is to cover up any flashes of tape that might possibly be seen as the cards are cut off of it.

"Your card, the Two of Hearts."

fig. 15   fig. 16

fig. 17   fig. 18

You will now switch out the taped pick for the finger-palmed pick that is below the cards in the right hand. To do so, lift your right thumb off of the taped pick and then turn the entire hand palm down, releasing the finger-palmed pick from under the cards in the right hand (fig. 17). Let the tossed pick fall onto the face-up selection on the face of the cards in the left hand. Be careful not to flash the pick on the underside of the cards in the right hand even though the front of these cards do provide an ample amount of cover (fig. 18).

"And that is how a rock star 'picks a card'."

Place the right-hand half of the deck with the taped pick securely hidden underneath it directly below the face-up cards in the left hand. Take the pick off of the selected card and place it into your right pocket.

"Gotta love the Manilow Magic Pick. Works every single time."

Grab ahold of the deck with both hands, as if you were going to throw it down in celebration, but use your right thumb to fold the taped pick back up under the face-up deck. Suddenly "come to your senses" and stop what you are doing. Gently cut the face-up deck, placing the taped pick card back into the center of the pack. Use your right thumb to riffle off the taped card, creating a thumb break above it. Cut one more time to the break and the taped card is now on the face of the deck.

"I feel like I should trash the deck like a real Rock God, but I just got this one…"

Reach into your pocket and bring out the card case, or pick it up from off of the table, if that is where you left it. Place the deck into the card case and you are reset for an encore performance.

> *"...so I'm sure you understand, right? Rock and roll!!"*

Put the cased deck away into your pocket as you scope out the crowd for any potential backstage pass candidates that may have been super-duper impressed with your "card guitar" antics. If none are available, you can certainly just put the deck away, be your own backstage groupie, and go to bed early...or just feel free to omit this last rock-and-roll step altogether.

Oh Yeah...

Talk about audience participation. Anytime you can get a spectator to throw down a vicious air guitar solo on a playing card...well, that's entertainment. For what it is worth, this effect can be performed with a coin, instead of a guitar pick, if that is the way you feel that you need to take it. I like using the pick because it's different, it's got the built-in "pick a card" pun, and let's face it, guitar players playing with picks are sexier than bank tellers playing with coins. A big rock-and-roll thank you to Jack Carpenter for helping me finesse some of the structure of this routine. One last thing: if you plan on doing more fun stuff with the pack after this effect, you could simply turn the deck face down at the conclusion and cop out the gimmicked card instead of putting the cards into the case. Now, go let your inner rock star shine.

Effect

A quarter is borrowed and initialed by the spectator. So as not to commit a first-class felony, some of the ink is removed with a Mister Clean Magic Eraser. This helpful household hint goes a little too far when the coin somehow gets absorbed deep inside of the eraser. The only way to get the coin out now is to rip it right out of Mister Clean's cold, torn, magic hands. How dramatic!!

Needed

A Mister Clean Magic Eraser. This is a cleaning sponge treated with some sort of wonderful "magic sauce" that is available at most grocery stores. Of course, any knock-off brand will do, but really, I tend to go with Mister Clean because he's got some serious style, right? You will also need a permanent black marker, a small knife or pair of scissors (optional), and of course, a borrowed quarter.

Preparation

Take the eraser and break it into two equal pieces. You will use and destroy each one of the halves every time that you perform this routine. A package usually comes with anywhere from two to four individual erasers, so you can get a decent number of performances for a just couple of dollars. Take one of the halves and cut a "U" shaped slit into the bottom of it (fig. 1). The diameter of this slit needs to be a little bit longer than the diameter

fig. 1

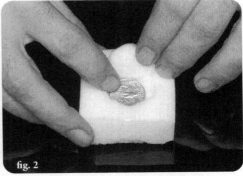
fig. 2

of the quarter. Feel free to use a knife or scissors to do the job, but in all honesty, these erasers are pliable enough that you can simply cut the slit into it with something like a coin, if needed. You will now turn that "U"-shaped cut into a "hinged" flap that will cover a "secret well". This is accomplished by simply scooping out some of the eraser that lies directly beneath the slit. This secret compartment needs to be deep enough to house a quarter completely inside of it (fig. 2). Close the flap and place the eraser, along with the marker, into your right pocket.

Performance

Approach a spectator that looks as if they have not done time in prison recently.

> *"Who wants to break the law? Anybody? Easy, easy!! One at a time! Wow!! My kinda audience."*

Borrow a quarter from the spectator and look it over as if you are checking it for any illegal markings.

> *"Can I please borrow a quarter? Did you know that is actually a felony to deface US currency? If you write on a coin, or a bill, or even a bar of gold, that is against the law—a federal law, at that. How exciting. I would like you to help me commit what actually may go down in history as the crime of the century."*

Place the quarter into your left hand so that you can remove the marker from your pocket with your right hand. Give the quarter and the marker to the spectator with instructions to write their initials on one side of the coin.

> *"Do me a favor. Take this marker and write down your initials on this coin. Don't worry. You won't be going to prison on my watch, OK?"*

Take the quarter back from the spectator and examine the markings up closely.

"Alright. You have just permanently marked the coin, essentially ruining it and taking out of circulation. The economy could crash, and it would all be your fault. I can see that you are starting to get a little nervous. I would be to."

Transfer the marker to the same hand that is holding the coin, temporarily clipping it between the middle and ring fingers (fig. 3). This will allow you to dip the fingers of your other hand into a glass of water, getting them wet enough to "try" to wipe off the permanent ink, but of course, you will fail miserably in this attempt. Or do what I do and just lick those fingers nice and good, soliciting the best "ewwww" moment you can get.

"Due to the permanent nature of the ink, it's on there forever, so basically, you're screwed."

Take the marker into your free but wet hand, and write your initials onto the other side of the quarter.

"Tell you what, let's live dangerously. I will be your accomplice and go down in flames with you. I'm signing my initials on the other side of the coin. We are so bad!!!"

Blow on both sides of the coin to ensure that the ink is dry, while again showing that the marked initials are permanently on there.

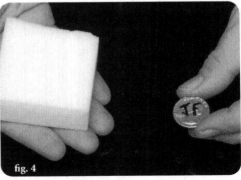

fig. 3   fig. 4

"Now, I don't know about you, but I'm not cut out for prison. I'm tender. Jail is definitely not my scene. So, when I do end up with illegally marked coins, I have a plan, a way out."

Place the marker back into your right pocket and then bring out the eraser with the slit side resting on your outstretched right palm (fig. 4).

"Of course, I use magic. Well, actually, I use one of these: a Magic Eraser. They are in all of the stores...and well, they ARE magic. Watch and I will show you exactly how we can get away it completely clean."

Hold the eraser in between your right thumb and fingertips, with the thumb above, and make a feeble attempt at wiping off the ink. The ink will not budge because the eraser is bone dry.

"An everyday double-marked coin and a little bit of magic...and it doesn't come off at all."

Wet your fingertips again, using your preferred method. Apply the moisture to the ink on the coin, wipe it with the eraser, and just like that...it comes off! Only wipe off about half of your set of initials, leaving the spectator's on the other side as well (fig. 5).

"But we add a little bit of wetness and...the ink is starting to come off of the coin."

Hand the quarter back to the spectator to show that your initials are indeed coming off, as well as to verify that their initials are still permanently on the other side.

"Take a look at the other side. Same coin. Nothing sneaky. Just good clean magic. Pretty amazing, huh?"

While the spectator is busy looking at the quarter, your left hand approaches the eraser from above and squeezes its long sides. This will cause the eraser to bow inward just enough for the flap to pop open underneath (fig. 6). The right hand scissor clips the flap between the index and middle fingers (fig. 7). Once the flap is clipped, hold the eraser in what is essentially right-hand dealer's grip. The flap on the underside of the eraser is completely hidden from view by the right index finger, so let's get down and dirty with this extremely clean vanish.

"To be honest, I hardly go anywhere without one of these in my back pocket. You just never know."

Have the spectator place the quarter back onto your palm-up left fingers.

"I suppose we better get to work on this side of the coin now."

Begin to rub the quarter vigorously with the eraser, stopping a few times to check on your ink-removal progress. After two or three of these checks, you

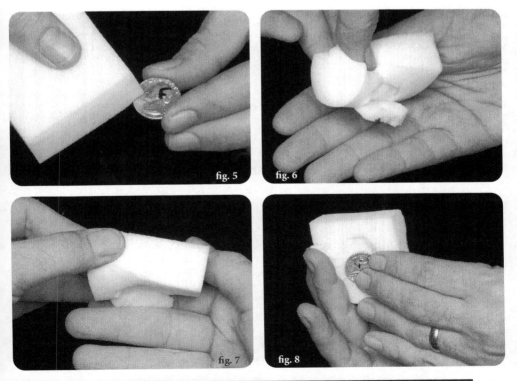

fig. 5

fig. 6

fig. 7

fig. 8

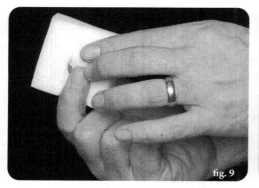
fig. 9

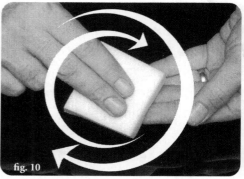
fig. 10

are going to make the quarter vanish by utilizing the most knuckle-busting, hardcore move I've ever developed. That's right, your left fingertips simply place the quarter right into the secret compartment underneath the eraser (fig. 8). This secret stealth maneuver is easily concealed by the larger action of the right hand's frantic scrubbing motions.

Once the coin has been tucked away into the hidden compartment, use your right index finger to close the flap back up into the eraser, which is also covered by the larger scrubbing movements (fig. 9).

"This one appears to have a little bit more ink, so we just need to rub a bit harder...I guess."

Stop scrubbing for just a second and rotate your right hand palm down, and immediately resume scrubbing the supposed quarter with the non-slit side of the eraser. Your right fingertips are covering the slit on top of the eraser (fig. 10). You will also reduce the risk of flashing by keeping the slit side angled away from the audience's line of vision during these final scrubs.

"I'll keep it right here at the fingertips so we can all see it. Here we go."

Slow down the scrubbing motion and slowly spread your left fingers apart from one another, concentrating the scrubbing eraser on just your left middle finger. Slowly lift the eraser from off of the tip of the left middle finger and look down at it, noticing that the quarter is now "gone" (fig. 11).

> *"And that should just about do it…. Oh wait. It's ummmm…gone."*

The spectator will always look to the left hand to see that the coin is gone and then they immediately shift their gaze back to the underside of the eraser, where there is no slit. This is a wonderful moment. Act confused as you show both sides of the eraser by revolving your right hand palm up and then back palm down. Your right fingers conceal the slit during this turnover sequence.

> *"That's completely weird."*

Pretend to mentally run through the steps you just took up to the point of vanishing the coin to see if you missed something. Suddenly realize what the problem is.

> *"Wait a second. I think that maybe we used too much magic…"*

Shake the eraser up toward the right ear, as if you could possibly hear something inside. Lower the eraser back down parallel to the floor, holding it between the thumb and fingers, thumb below.

> *"…and the eraser actually absorbed the coin inside."*

To produce the quarter from within the eraser, you are basically going to use the classic "Coin In Bread Roll" move, which I originally learned in

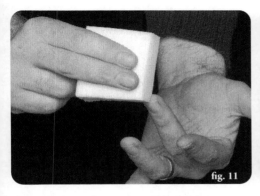

fig. 11

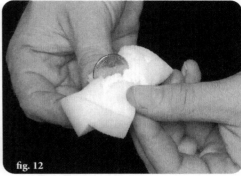

fig. 12

Mulholland's Book of Magic by John Mulholland (1963), although I'm sure it's been around since before the days of sliced bread. Basically, the left hand mirrors the right hand's grip on the eraser, so that both thumbs are in position to push the quarter up and through the eraser, breaking it into two (fig. 12). Extend the quarter that is now sticking out from the center of the two broken halves toward the spectator to confirm that it is their signed coin. This is a very visual display, so milk it good.

> *"Let's take a look. Wow, there it is!! Look! Inside of the Magic Eraser! Your signed coin! That... is some serious magic."*

Once the coin has been removed, you are going to diffuse the gimmick by completing the tear along the secret slit. All evidence has been destroyed except, of course, for their initials on the coin. At this point, I give them a little piece of the eraser to take with them "to clean up the crime scene", as I suspiciously look around to make sure that the coast is clear.

> *"Here, do yourself a favor. Take this piece of eraser and don't tell anybody you got it from me. Get that mark off of there when you can. I think somebody may be watching us. Got it? Good."*

Oh Yeah...

This is a lot of fun. I have always performed the Coin in Roll effect, but why, oh why, does a coin appear there? I like how this presentation makes sense. Plus, you get the extra-added bonus of a practical way to get the ink off all of your illegally marked coins. Here's a helpful hint. Make sure to keep the flap of the hidden well thick enough, especially around the hinge, so that it doesn't accidentally come off during one of your more over-enthusiastic performances.

Jacked Up

Joe Cole

Effect

The overzealous magician makes an unprepared attempt to cut to a previously selected card, such as the Queen of Spades. After failing miserably, a wickedly-clean "Twisting the Jacks"-type of smoke and mirrors is performed. In an attempt to save some face, real magic takes over as the four "twisted" Jacks all change into the very same suit as the selected card. The magic quotient gets cranked all the way up as those four jacks suddenly transform into 4/5ths of a Royal Flush. The deck is then triumphantly spread and in the center is the spectator's selected face-up Queen of Spades, which just so happens to be the fifth and final card needed to complete that flush of the royal variety!

Needed

A deck of cards, some double-stick tape, and a double-face card with the Ten of Spades on one side and the Jack of Hearts on the other. Two of these cards can be found in a deck of double-facers, available at most magic stores. Of course, you can also glue a regular Ten and Jack together and make your own double-facer, if that is how you choose to roll.

Preparation

Place a small piece of double-stick tape, no bigger than half of the size of your fingernail, onto the face of the regular Jack of Hearts from the deck. The tape will camouflage very nicely into the busy ink on the center of the card. It will help out later if you dull the tape's stickiness a bit by adhering it to a piece of your clothing a few times.

OK, now go through the deck and remove the Ace of Spades, the King of Spades, and the Jack of Spades. Add these three cards to the double-facer and the taped Jack of Hearts. Set all five of the cards in the following order, from top to bottom: the face-up, taped Jack of Hearts, the face-down Ace of Spades, the face-down King of Spades, the face-down Jack of Spades, and the double-face card, with the Jack of Hearts side facing up (fig. 1). Place this packet, with the face-up Jack of Hearts outermost, underneath the cellophane that is wrapped around the card box. If you have other plans for your card box that don't involve cellophane, then you can simply put these cards into your pocket until you need to bring them out.

Performance

While you are being witty, go through the deck and cut the Queen of Spades to the top of the pack.

"Alright. They say practice makes perfect so here goes nothing. I've been working on this trick for like, forever; at least five or six… minutes. But I'm game if you are. Let's do it."

You will need to force this Queen upon your spectator. A good, old-fashioned riffle force will make the grade for you.

"Go ahead and say 'stop' as I riffle down through the deck like this. Ready?"

To perform a riffle force, cut the Queen back into the center of the pack, but hold a pinky break above it. As the deck is held in left-hand dealer's

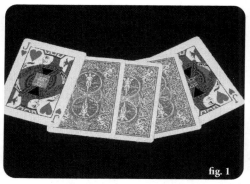

fig. 1

fig. 2

grip, riffle down the upper left corner of the deck with the thumb until the spectator says, "Stop." Try and time the riffle so that the spectator says "stop" somewhere near your pinky break. You will not actually separate the cards where the spectator indicates. Instead, using your right hand from above, lift up all of the cards above the pinky break by their front and back edges. The savvy reader will recognize this position as Biddle Grip.

"Excellent. You've done this before, I see."

Extend the left-hand portion of cards toward the spectator as you push the forced Queen to the right with your left thumb.

"Take a look at the card that you have selected."

Allow the Queen to be noted by the spectator as you turn your head away so that you cannot see the card's identity.

"Keep it to yourself. I don't want to know what it is."

Once the Queen has been "selected" and remembered, use your left thumb to pull it back flush with the bottom half of the pack. Place the right-hand cards back onto the cards in the left hand, holding a pinky break above the Queen.

"And now we return it into the pack from which it came. I know. How dramatic, right?"

You will now control this Queen to the top of the pack by any method you see fit; a double undercut is as good as any other method. To perform, transfer the pinky break to the right thumb as the entire deck is taken into right-hand Biddle Grip. With your left hand, take half of the cards below the thumb break and place them on top of the deck (fig. 2). Repeat the action with the rest of the cards below the thumb break, transferring them to the top of the deck. This brings the "selected" Queen up to the top of the pack, which is exactly where you need to be.

fig. 3   fig. 4

"I shall now do the 'impossible'. Okay, maybe not the 'impossible', but definitely the 'moderately, above-average' act of cutting directly to your card. This task would be difficult enough to do even if I knew exactly where the card was in the deck. But since right now I really have no idea, imagine the inner panic that is racing through my soul. You like that, don't you?"

Under the guise of attempting to cut to the Queen, you will secretly be reversing it into the center of the deck by means of the Braue Reversal. This is a very easy and efficient way of accomplishing this task.

"Well, here goes nothing."

To perform, hold the deck in left-hand dealer's grip as your right hand approaches from above in Biddle Grip position. With your right thumb, lift up the back edge of the top card (Queen of Spades) in order to hold a left pinky break below it. Momentarily let go of the deck with the left hand as the break is taken over by the right thumb. Take the bottom half of the deck into left-hand dealer's grip, as your right hand continues holding the top half with a thumb break below the Queen. Turn your left hand palm down, bringing the cards face up in the process, and ask if this cut-to card on the bottom of the deck is their "selected" card.

"Your card, the Four of Clubs?"

After the spectator says that it is not, place these cards face up on top of the card above the break in the right hand (fig. 3).

"No? No problem. We shall call that a 'test run'."

Next, take all of the cards below the thumb break into left-hand dealer's grip, rotate the cards face up, and ask again if this bottom card is their selected card.

"Your card, the Nine of Hearts?"

After they say "no", place these cards face up underneath the right-hand cards (fig. 4). The Queen is now reversed in the center of the deck, and that...is the Braue Reversal.

"No?"

You are now going to act as if you genuinely messed it up, but first, a quick rant on the "Magician-in-Trouble" scenario. Subtlety is key here. Think about the times when a routine really has gone awry. I'm sure you had more of an internal dialog about how you were feeling at the time, as opposed to acting as if you were seriously in trouble. Our first reaction is usually to try and "wing it" and get through it somehow, someway. You rarely see a magician break down in tears when it all goes south, as fun as that actually may be to see. Usually their wheels start turning as they look for the quickest way to cover the mistake. Just be charming, witty, and "quick on your feet". That's the attitude your "Magician-in-Trouble" bit should have, not one of sheer panic. If you go too far with it, nobody will believe it.

"So, it looks like I jacked that one up pretty good, huh?"

Table the deck face down and stall for a moment, as if you were trying to come with some way to smoothly get out of this.

"Well, I'm going to try to save some face here, what little face I have left."

Suddenly, act as if you have just figured out how to play this one off and then remove the special packet of cards that you set aside earlier.

> *"Wait, I actually know exactly what to do here."*

You will have to separate the taped Jack of Hearts on the bottom from the rest of the cards in the packet. This is not a move. You just pop that taped sucker free by pulling up on all of the cards above it. Once done, place the taped Jack face up on top of the packet, which you now should be holding in left-hand dealer's grip.

> *"Anytime I 'jack up' a trick like that, I need to make up for it somehow and that's why I have these."*

You will now show the packet of cards in your right hand as four face-up Jacks of Hearts. This is accomplished by performing an amazing move of Brother John Hamman's called the Hamman Count from *The Card Magic of Brother John Hamman S.M.* by Paul LePaul (1958).

To perform: The right hand reaches over and momentarily re-grips the packet by the short ends in Biddle Grip. With your left thumb, slide the taped Jack of Hearts back into left-hand dealer's grip for the count of "one". As your hands come back together to apparently peel the next Jack into the left hand, all of the right-hand cards get wedged into the fork of the left thumb. As that is happening, the right thumb and ring-finger take the single Jack back to the right for the count of "two" (fig. 5). This exchange should really look as if you simply were counting the second card into the left hand. For the count of "three", repeat the mechanics of the previous exchange, but this time, place the single Jack into the fork of the left thumb as you take the packet back with the right hand. For the count of "four", place the single Jack in your left hand back on top of the packet in the right hand. You have very effectively shown four face-up Jacks of Hearts, and you are definitely a better person for it.

"Check it out. Four ordinary Jacks of Hearts, stolen from four other magicians' decks. Now, when do I 'jack-up' the magic, I bring these guys in to reverse the damage. That's right. These cards will go 'jack-down'."

You will now make each of the jacks turn face-down, utilizing an excellent bit of routining from Gary Freed's extremely kickin' marketed effect, "NFW".

Hold the right edge of the packet between your right fingertips and thumb, fingers underneath. You are going to make the first jack turn face down with a trusty Elmsley Count, which is taught in detail in "Well Traveled" in this very book. But for the sake of completeness, here's a brief description to get you rolling. The left thumb takes the top card into left-hand dealer's position ("one"). The right thumb pushes off all of the cards above the bottom one into the left hand, while simultaneously the right fingers steal back the single card in the left hand beneath the solo bottom card in the right hand ("two"). The right thumb then pushes its top card onto the left-hand packet ("three"). Lastly, the final card in the right hand is then placed on top of the left-hand packet ("four"). This will show one card face down.

"All you have to do is say 'jack-down', and just like that, one of the Jacks of Hearts turns face down."

To make the second Jack turn face down, square up the cards and perform another Elmsley Count, exactly as before. This will show that the two middle cards are now face down.

fig. 5

fig. 6

Place the packet into the left-hand dealing position and spread the top three cards to the right with the left thumb. Once again, you are displaying a face-up Jack of Hearts, two face-down cards, and another face-up Jack of Hearts (fig. 6). In between the thumb and fingers of the right hand, take these top three cards a little bit to the right, while at the same time, your left thumb reaches over and slides off the top card of the three (taped Jack of Hearts) onto the face-up Jack in the left hand (fig. 7). Place the face-down cards in the right hand underneath the packet in the left hand.

"...and amazingly, he turns face down, too."

Now it's time for the third card to go face down. Ask the spectator to snap their fingers to make the next "Jack" do its turning thing.

"Third one? Well, this one is just downright crazy. Watch in full view as it turns 'jack-down' when you snap your fingers. Are you ready? Do it."

When they make their magic move, turn the face-up Jack of Hearts face down slowly and deliberately. This will get the desired laugh/groan that you would expect, but also does the dirty work for you by placing the taped Jack face-to-face with the other one, preparing you for the fourth and final Jack's turnover. Give the packet a gentle squeeze from above and below to ensure that the double-stick tape does its sticky stuff.

fig. 7

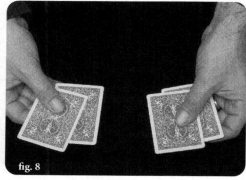
fig. 8

"I know, I know. Bad joke. But while you were busy not laughing..."

To make the fourth Jack turn face down, simply spread the cards. Four face-down cards are displayed. This is an extremely strong and powerful moment.

"...the fourth Jack turned 'jack-down' as well. Four 'jack-downs'. I feel a little bit better about this now, don't you?"

"Realize" that you still need to find their selected card in order to be the magic maker that you have always strived to be.

"But I know what you're saying. You are saying, 'That's all fine and dandy, but you never did find my card.' Well, that is true and so very nice of you to point that out."

Take the top two cards of the spread with your right hand, displaying two cards in each hand (fig. 8).

"Well, these Jacks don't just turn face down. Believe it or not, they can actually tell me the suit of the very card that you selected."

fig. 9

Wave the two cards in the right hand over the deck like a little "card-shaped magic wand". When you are done being mystical, place these two cards on top of the left-hand packet.

"All I have to do is wave them over the deck like this and..."

Pick up the packet in right-hand Biddle Grip, turn your hand palm up, and show the bottom card. Amazingly, this Jack of Hearts has turned into the Jack of Spades, identifying the selected card's suit (fig. 9).

> *"...this Jack of Hearts turns into the Jack of Spades, which I think means that your card was a Spade."*

But you are not done yet. You are going to show that all of the cards have now turned into Jacks of Spades. This is accomplished with The Flushtration Count, a move that is used to show the back or face of a card repeatedly as several different cards. Brother John Hamman popularized the move in his marketed trick, "Flushtration", in 1969, but it was actually originally published by Norman Houghton in *Ibidem*, No. 1 (1955).

The Flushtration Count is performed as follows: after showing the Jack of Spades on the face of the packet, turn your hand palm down so you are holding the cards from above in right-hand Biddle Grip. The left thumb slides the top card (the taped double) into left-hand dealer's grip, miscalling it as the first Jack of Spades. The right hand then rotates palm up and shows the bottom card of the packet again, which of course is the same Jack of Spades that was just previously shown, but the audience will believe that it is another one (fig. 10). Turn the packet face down and use your left thumb to slide off this new top card (the second "Jack") into the left hand. Repeat this action of turning palm up to display, followed by turning palm down as the top card is peeled off to show the third "Jack". Finally turn your right hand palm up, displaying the fourth Jack, which you then place face down onto the others in the left hand. This count should be performed at a brisk "1, 2, 3, 4" pace.

fig. 10

fig. 11

"And so does this one, and this one, and this one. Very interesting."

Holding the packet face down in left-hand dealing position, use your left thumb to spread the top two cards over to the right, and then cut them to the face of the packet.

"Not bad, huh? Not bad for a trick that started off being completely 'jacked-up'. 'Royally jacked-up' is more like it. And since I still haven't officially found your card, I'll use these cards now to royally find yours."

Turn the cards face up to reveal the Ten of Spades on the face of the packet.

"This one tells me you weren't thinking of the Ten."

Deal the Ten of Spades (which is actually two cards held together with double-stick tape) onto the right side of the table. Next, deal the Jack of Spades onto the Ten, but jogged to the left. This will help cover the thickness of the Ten of Spades.

"This one tells me you weren't thinking of the Jack."

Next, the King of Spades is dealt onto the left side of the table, followed by the Ace, which is placed on top of the King in the same side-jogged fashion as the cards on the right side of the table (fig. 11).

"Or the King or even the Ace. And speaking of 'royal', that's almost a Royal Flush. All except for..."

After showing that the selected card wasn't one of the tabled cards, spread the face-down deck (preferably right to left), revealing the Queen of Spades face up in the deck.

"...your selected card, the Queen of Spades!"

Pick up the four-tabled cards, hold them in a small, face-up fan, and then openly place the Queen in between the Jack and the King for your well-deserved moment of glory (fig. 12).

fig. 12

"It's a royal success. I know what you are thinking. You are thinking, 'That's soooo "jacked-up",' and you know what? You're soooo right. Royally."

As you clean up, casually show the backs of the cards. If you are not doing walk around, place this fan together with the rest of the deck, box them up, and then move on to more important matters. If you would like to reset the trick, this can easily be done right in front of the audience. Simply take the Queen of Spades and place it back into the deck. Square the fan with the right hand from above, holding the cards by their edges. The left-hand fingers separate the Jack of Hearts from the bottom of the packet. The left hand will now openly transfer this Jack to the top of the packet (on top of the Ace), turning it face down in the process. The cards are now reset. Place them face down underneath the cellophane or back into the pocket and you are ready for your next "Jacked-Up" performance.

Oh Yeah...

This routine has A LOT of magic happening. A selected card gets found, the Jacks turn face down one at a time, the Jacks turn into the selected card's suit, à la Hofzinser Ace style, and of course, the sudden transformation into a Royal Flush. Four separate magical effects! What a bargain!! But wait, there's more!!! For those out there just begging for one more effect to cram into this kickin' routine, Joe sometimes throws in a color-changing kicker as well.

Basically, replace all of the red-backed cards in your secret Jack/Royal Flush packet with blue-backed cards. Now, place a face-up blue-backed Queen of Spades second from the top in the deck. Start with the regular red-backed Queen on the face of the deck. Cut the deck and hold a break below the red-backed Queen of Spades now in the center. Lift up all of the cards above the break when the spectator says so and display this forced Queen. Replace the top half of the cards and you are good to go. The card has been forced and there is now a duplicate blue-backed Queen face up in the center. Just cut around it when you are pretending to try to cut directly to their "selected" card. Now, when you bring out the blue-backed "Jack" packet, just proceed as previously explained. When the time comes to reveal the reversed Queen in the deck, you can dramatically slide it out of the pack and turn it over to reveal that it really does belong to the Royal Flush packet because it, too, has a blue back.

Effect

An uncut key is visually cut into shape with nothing more than a little ink, a little bit of fire, and a whole lot of pizazz.

Needed

Two matching keys, one cut and one uncut (fig. 1). Simply go to your local hardware store and ask them for two matching keys and to then cut one of them for you. You will also need a black marker, a piece of flash paper, a black cigarette lighter, a small pair of sharp scissors, and a re-positionable glue stick or rubber cement.

Preparation

OK, I will admit that this is going to be the most labor-intensive preparation of any of the routines in the book. The good news is that we will make multiple copies of the gimmick at one shot, which actually saves time in the end. Before we dive into the preparation you will want a crash course in Key Anatomy 101. For purposes of explanation, refer to the pictured chart for the correct key-part terminology (fig. 2).

Take the cut key, place it on top of the piece of flash paper, and then line up the tip of the key on the bottom left corner of the paper. Take the marker and draw a line across the paper that starts about two centimeters above the shoulder stop of the key (fig. 3). The height of this line should be just over an inch or so from the bottom of the paper.

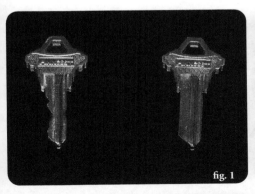

fig. 1

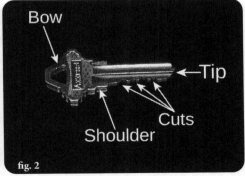

fig. 2

Bow

←Tip

Cuts

Shoulder

Now, make a series of accordion-style folds across the entire length of the paper. Each fold should be about a quarter of an inch apart from one another. You should be able to get around five to six folds per piece of paper (fig. 4). Once each section has been folded over upon itself, you will have a nice neat little package ready to be cut (fig. 5).

Take the scissors and carefully cut out a series of jagged, triangular cuts along the right side of the folded package (fig. 6). Note that the bases of the triangles are along the right side of the paper and that they extend all of the way up to the drawn line. We shall refer to these pieces of cut paper as the "paper teeth". If you open up the piece of paper flat, you will notice that there are now little diamond shapes on each of the folds.

Next, take the piece of paper and color everything below the black line completely black with the marker (fig. 7). The ink may bleed through after only coloring one side, but it would probably benefit you to color both sides of the paper regardless. You do not want any trace of white paper poking through.

Use the scissors to make a cut up each of the folds, also stopping at the drawn line (fig. 8). You will notice that every other cut bisects a diamond fold, leaving you with a piece of paper that now contains multiple sets of "paper teeth" (fig. 9). Whenever you are ready to perform this routine, simply cut off one of the sets of "paper teeth".

fig. 3

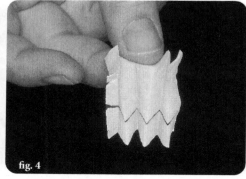

fig. 4

Take this cut-off set and trim off the top half of the "non-teeth" side, leaving you with a set of "paper teeth" ready to be glued into place.

Lastly, place a small dab of the glue on the shoulder stop of the cut key, as well as on the part of the blade that slants inward toward the tip (fig. 10). Carefully place the "paper teeth" across the length of the blade, so that the "paper teeth's" top edge is even with the top

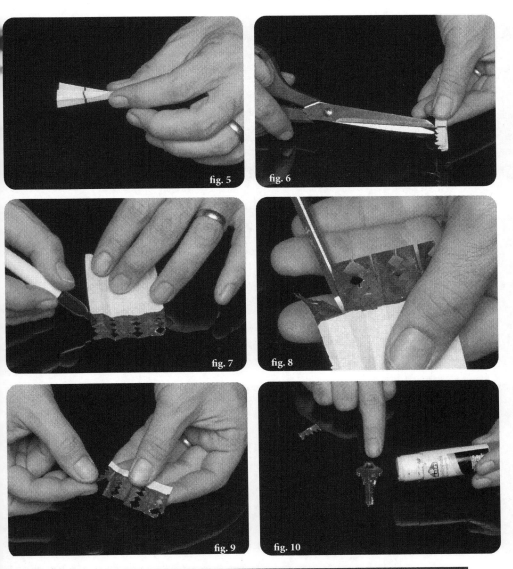

fig. 5

fig. 6

fig. 7

fig. 8

fig. 9

fig. 10

edge of the shoulder stop of the key. Trim away any excess piece of "paper teeth" that extends past the place where the blade slants toward the tip (fig. 11). The "paper teeth" should completely cover the actual teeth of the cut key (fig. 12).

Carefully place the prepared cut key and the marker into your left pants pocket. Place the uncut key and the lighter into your right pocket and you are ready to begin the routine.

Performance

Bring out the uncut key from your right pocket, holding its head between your right thumb and index finger.

> *"I'd like to show you a pretty cool optical illusion. Take a look at this. It's an uncut key, a piece of solid metal. What I like about it is that it's kind of like a blank slate, a wide-open world of opportunity, a galaxy of never-ending possibilities."*

Transfer the key to your left fingertips as you continue to display.

> *"OK, maybe I'm getting a little carried away here."*

Hand the uncut key to your spectator to take a look at.

> *"Michelangelo used to say that the sculpture is already there inside of the piece of rock and all he had to do was chisel away until it revealed itself."*

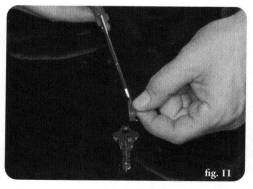

fig. 11

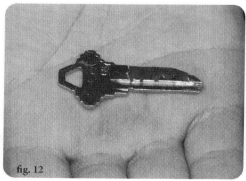

fig. 12

Suddenly look the spectator right in the eye and deliver the next line as if it were something of great importance that "they just had to know".

> *"That's Michelangelo, the artist, NOT Michelangelo the Teenage Mutant Ninja Turtle. Just so we are clear on that. I don't really know what the Ninja Turtles philosophies on art are, but I'm sure they are pretty awesome, too."*

Point to the uncut key with you right index finger as your left hand goes into the left pocket in preparation to bring out the marker.

> *"I kind of believe that every key has a predetermined series of cuts already inside of it. We just have to find them with a little magic..."*

While you are in the pocket, secretly grab ahold of the prepared cut key and place it into finger palm, so that the prepared side is away from your skin and the head of the key is closest to the left index finger. It is not terribly difficult to maneuver the key into this position while inside of the pocket. Just be careful not to let your left fingers feel around so much that they accidentally knock the glued piece of paper off of the key. Once the key is in the properly palmed position, grab the marker and bring it out of your pocket to display (fig. 13).

> *"...and a little bit of ink."*

Take back the uncut key from the spectator and maneuver it into a palm-up finger palm in the right hand, openly displaying it. It should be positioned

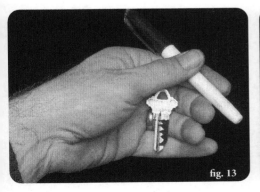

fig. 13

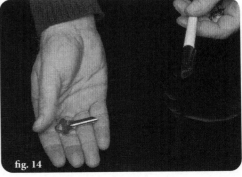

fig. 14

with its head toward the right index finger with the uncut edge pointing toward your body (fig. 14).

"Here's where the optical illusion comes into play."

We are going to switch out the uncut key for the prepared cut key under the guise of momentarily placing the marker in between your teeth so that you can transfer the key to your left hand, freeing up the right hand to write with.

So, here's how it goes down. Place the cap side of the marker in between your teeth with your left hand. Lower your left hand, still concealing the finger-palmed prepared key, so that it is about chest height, with the back of the hand facing the spectator. Place your right thumb on top on the key in the right hand, as if it were going to get ready to push the key to the fingertips as you raise the right hand up and behind the left-hand fingertips (fig. 15). The left hand pretends to take right-hand key. As you do so, the left thumb slides the prepared key's head up and over the top edge of the left index finger, where the spectator can now see it (fig. 16). As soon as the head of the key makes its appearance, raise your right hand, now concealing the uncut key in finger palm, up to the marker and pull it out from the cap being held between the teeth. Twirl the marker end for end between your right thumb and first two fingers. This is easy to do while palming the key. Insert the back of the marker back into the cap and then remove the marker from between your teeth, holding it in writing position in your right hand.

"I'm going to use this marker to black out some of the uncut key from view, like this."

Pretend to draw on the blade of the prepared key as the left hand continues to hold it in a neck-tied position, with just the very tip of the head exposed (fig. 17). As you lower the left hand down so that the prepared key can now be seen, you can actually color a bit of the flash paper for a little extra realism. Just don't get carried away and "color" the "paper teeth" right off of the key.

"Now, if you squint your eyes, it starts looking a little bit more like a real key. No?"

Again, raise the marker to your mouth and bite off the cap between your teeth. Twirl the marker end for end, just as before, and then replace the tip of it back into the cap between your teeth.

Remove the marker from your mouth with your right hand and place it into your right pocket, along with the finger-palmed key. Focus your attention on the key in the left hand as you put away the marker.

"How about if you spin around six times and shut your eyes painfully tight, then it starts to look a bit more like a cut key. No?"

Hold the key by its head in your left hand, displaying it at chest height.

"How about if you swallowed a whole bunch of magic mushrooms and stared right into the sun for about an hour? Maybe? Well, that might be a little extreme."

fig. 15

fig. 16

fig. 17

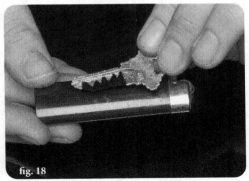
fig. 18

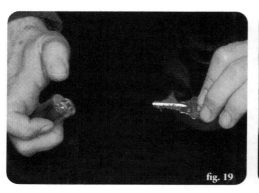

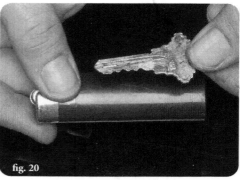

Reach into your right pocket and bring out the lighter.

"How about if we hold it up against something black, like this lighter?"

Hold the lighter horizontally behind the blade of the prepared key (fig. 18).

"See how the ink drawn on the key starts to blend in with the background? It kind of looks like it has been cut. A little? Maybe?"

Take the lighter out from behind the key and hold it "lighting" position in your right hand.

"Tough crowd. It's just an optical illusion. But, if we wanted to make it look like the real thing…"

Ignite the lighter and bring it toward the tip of the key.

"…we would just need to soften the metal a bit with a little fire. Watch!!!!"

Touch the flame to the end of the "paper teeth" closest to the tip of the key and watch it burn (fig. 19). The small moving flash that burns across the key, combined with the sudden appearance of real cut teeth, is some extremely visual stuff.

"What was once just a lame optical illusion has now become the genuine real thing, a solid metal cut key."

Place the lighter back into your right pocket and then use the nails of the right fingertips to scrape off any bits of flash paper that may not have ignited, due to being glued down. This is not a major deal. You just cut a freaking key with fire. There is bound to be some black ash or smeared ink left after that little miracle. So just pick it off and then hold it in front of the lighter to show the newly fire-cut teeth (fig. 20). Hand the key right back to the spectator to examine.

> *"A solid metal cut key that unlocks the front door to your house. Amazing, huh?"*

Take the key back from the spectator and triumphantly put it into your pocket, just like a good key cutter should.

> *"I'm just kidding about it unlocking your door, or am I? Maybe you should go ahead and change your lock, just to be on the safe side."*

Oh Yeah...

This is such a great illusion for one of those ever-popular TV spots, but that does not make it impractical to do in the real world. Knock out a few of those gimmicks all at once, and you will be ready to burn. Now, why not color the entire big piece of flash paper black before cutting it? Through experience, I have found that it is simply easier to see where you are making the cuts when the paper is white. If you have no difficulty with such arts and crafts challenges, then by all means, color away before you cut.

KILL YOUR CARDS

You can bend them, fold them, cut them, tear them.
Color them, squish them, squash them, flare them.
Slice them, dice them, draw them, throw them.
Eat them, beat them, burn them, blow them.
Break them, maim them, hurt them, use them.
Impail them, heave them, hide them, lose them.
It's best to impress an audience at rest and leave them wanting some more.
So kill your cards and they'll drop their guards without any jail time in store.

Kill your cards!